Fox

Coloring Book For Kids

Ages 3-12

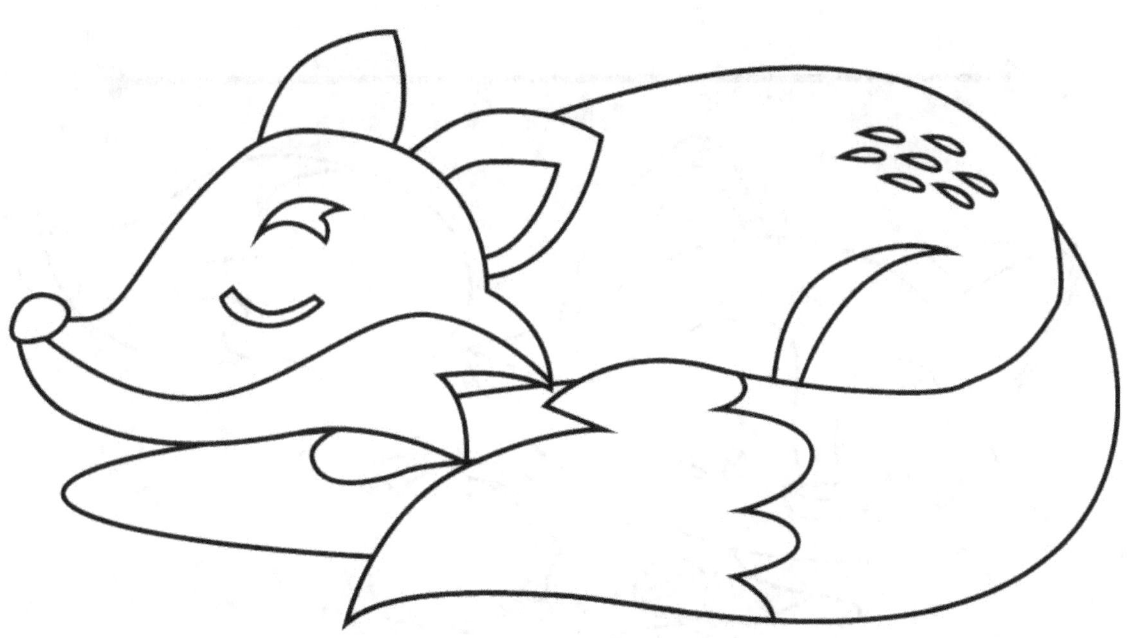

This Book Belongs To

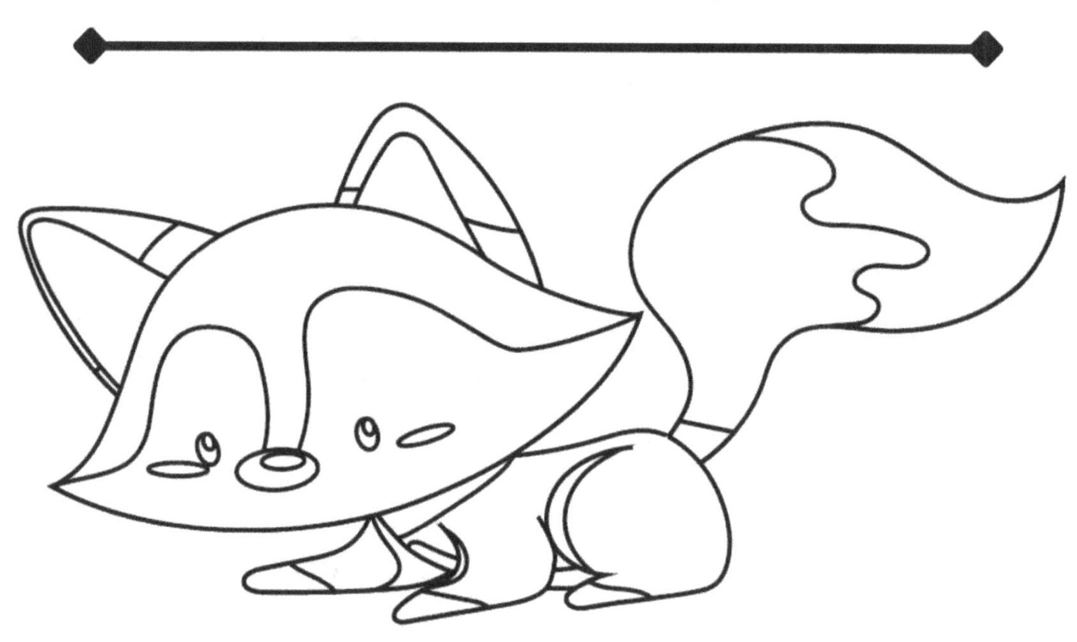

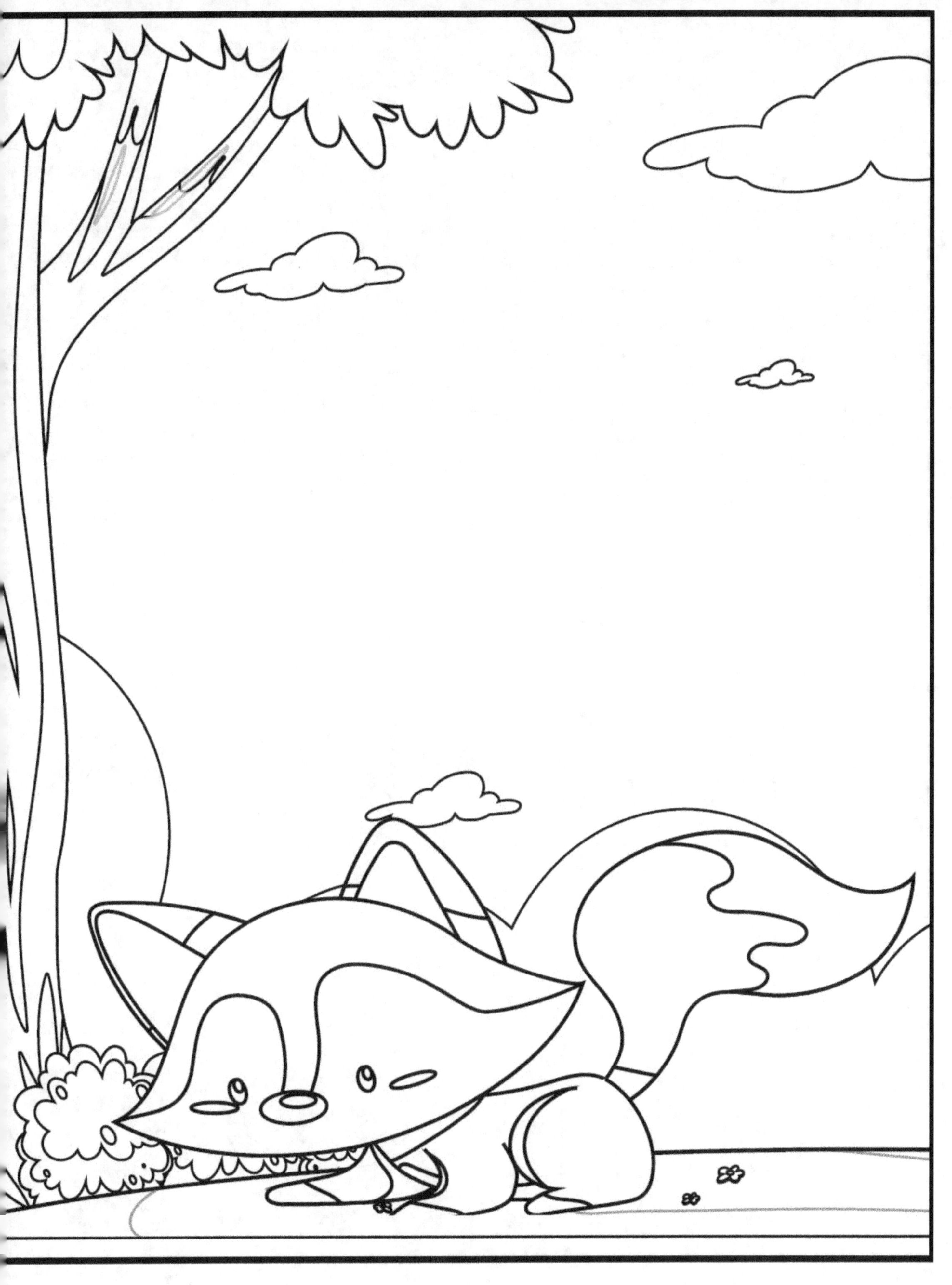

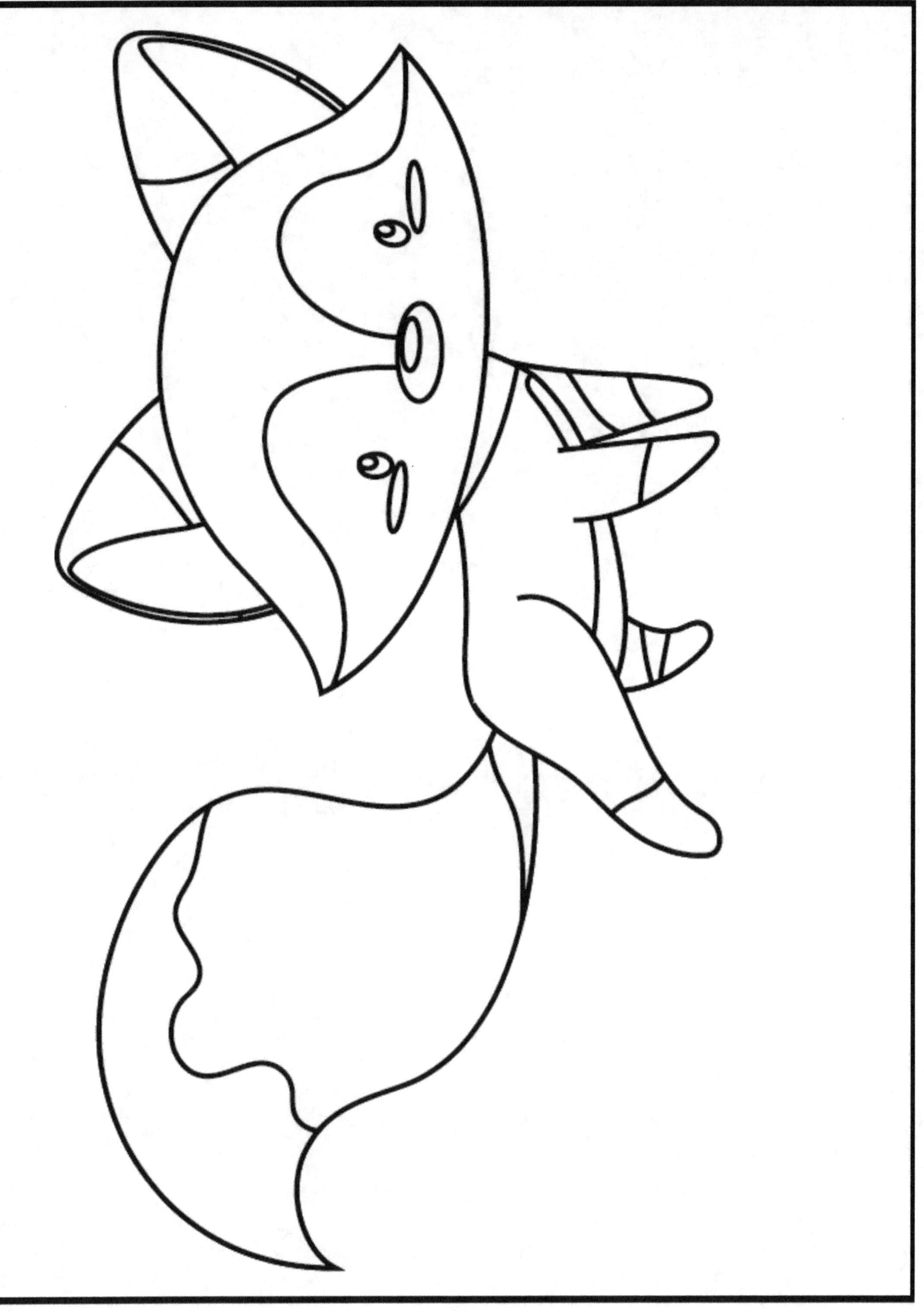

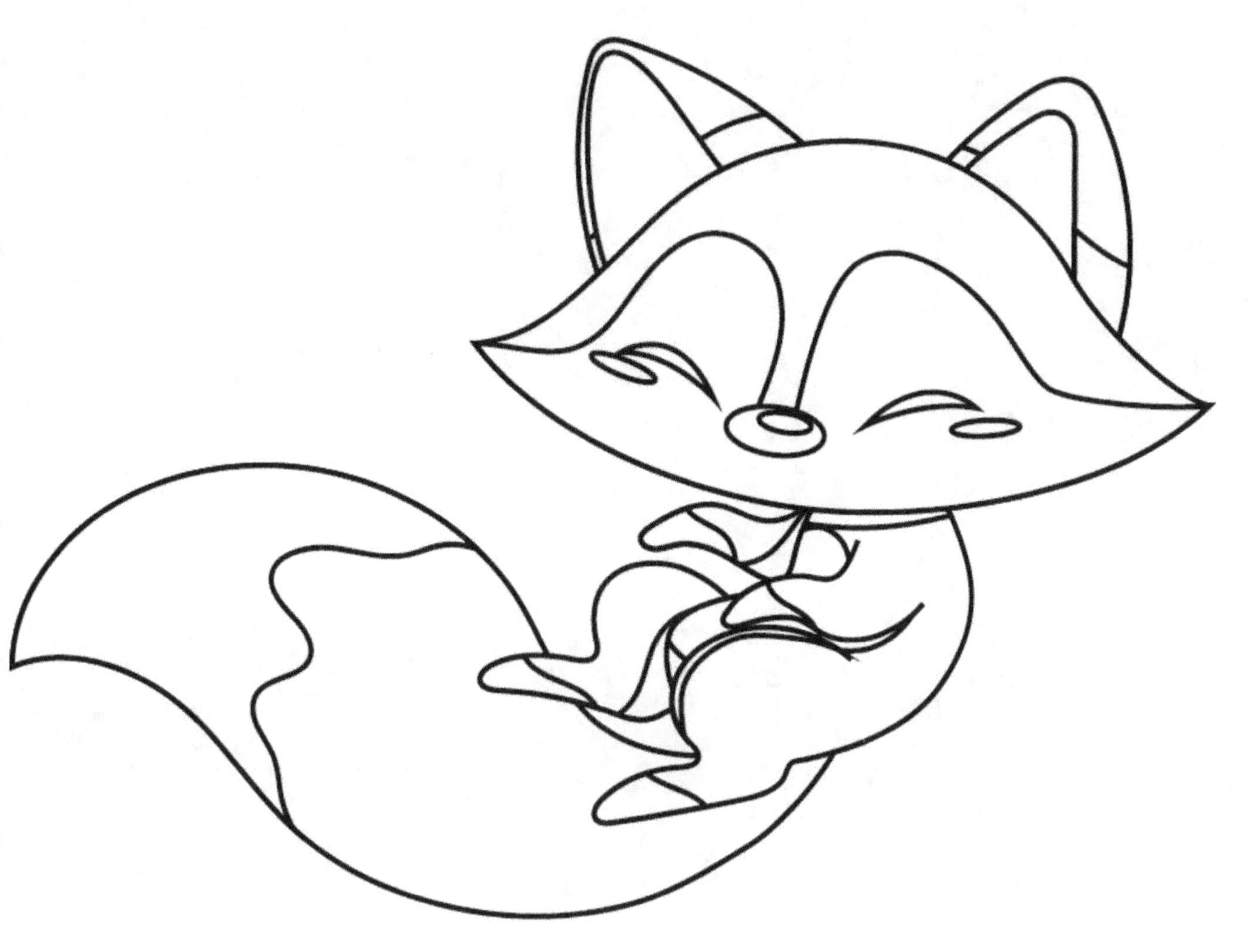

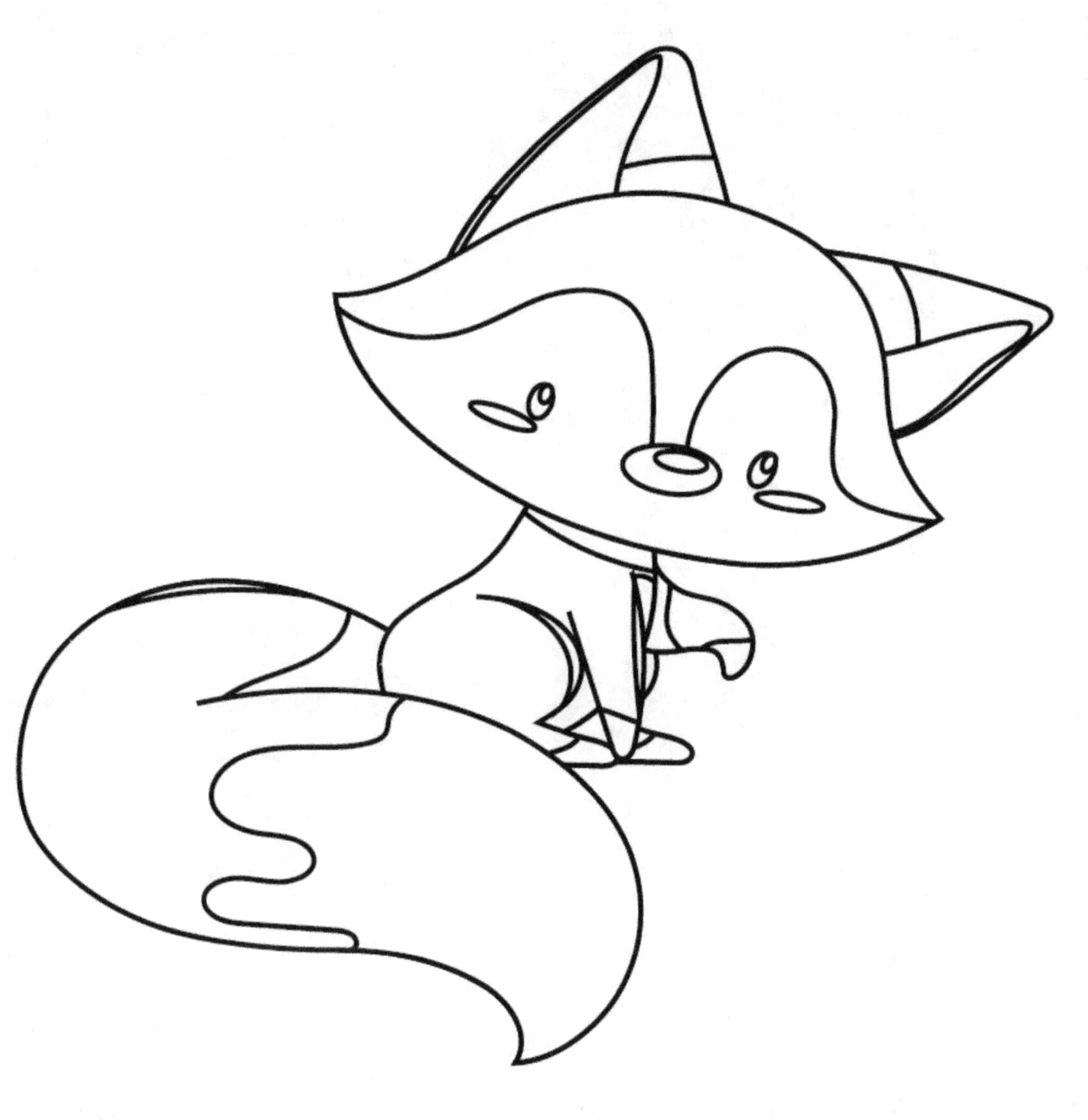

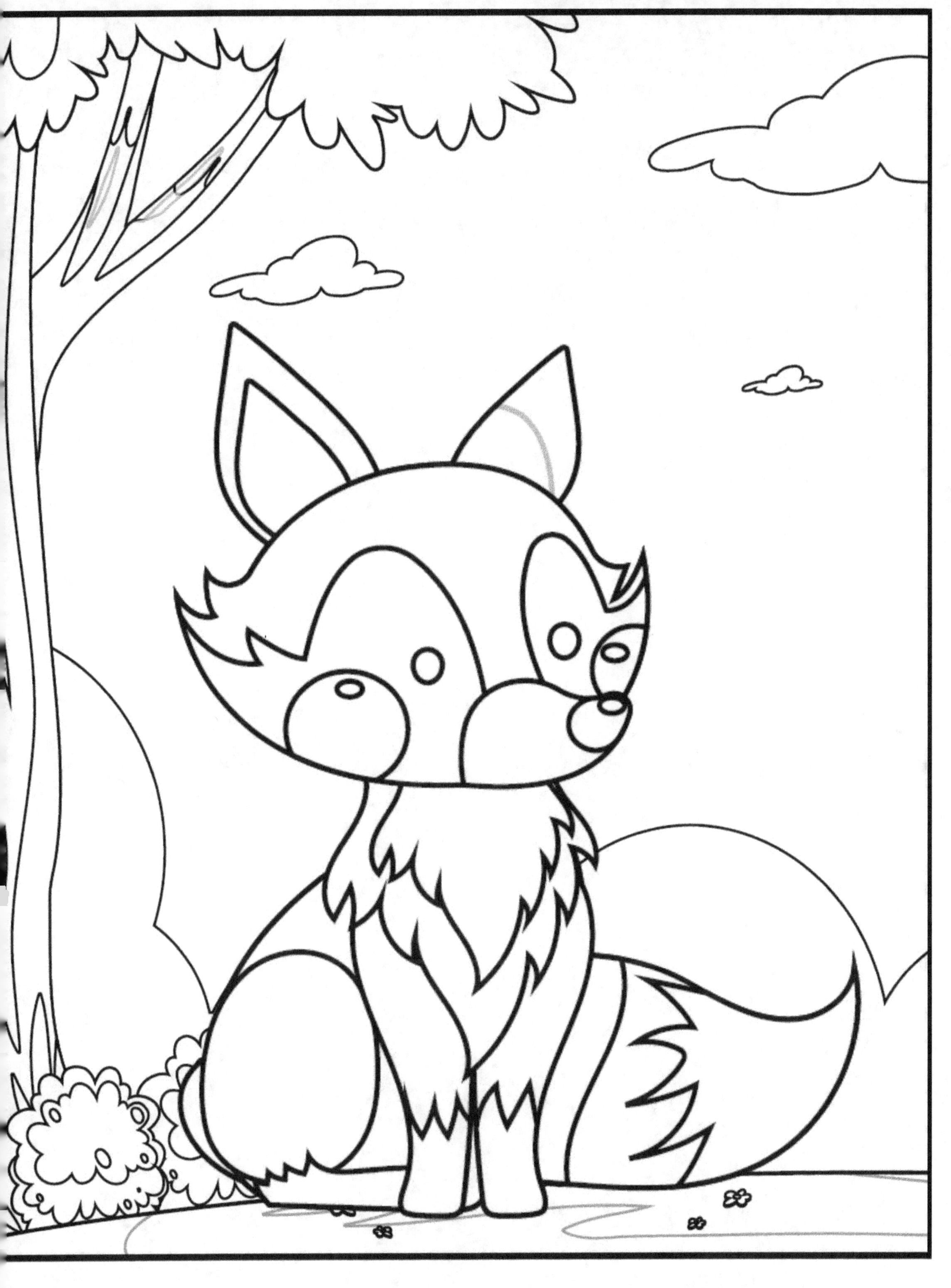

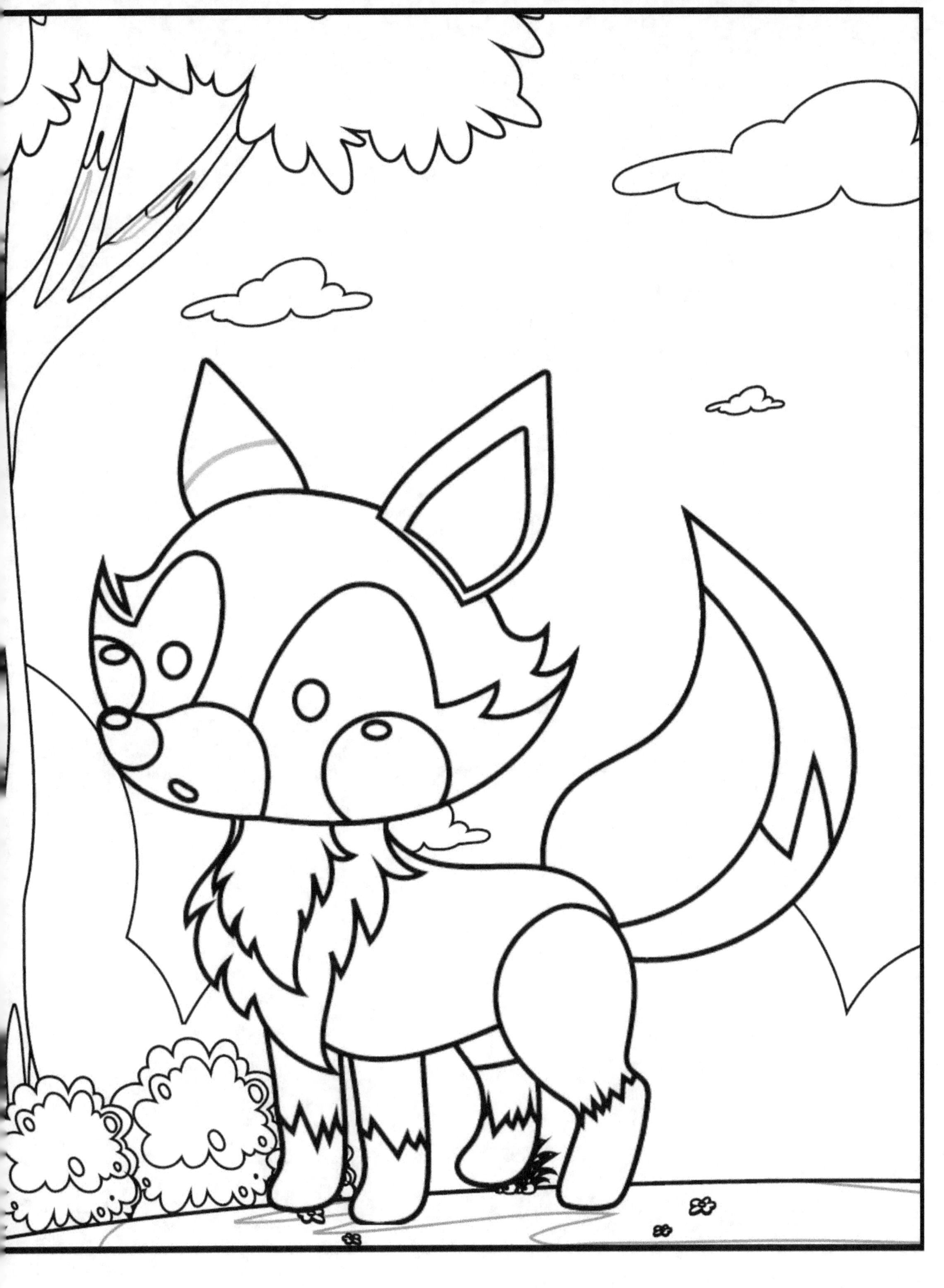

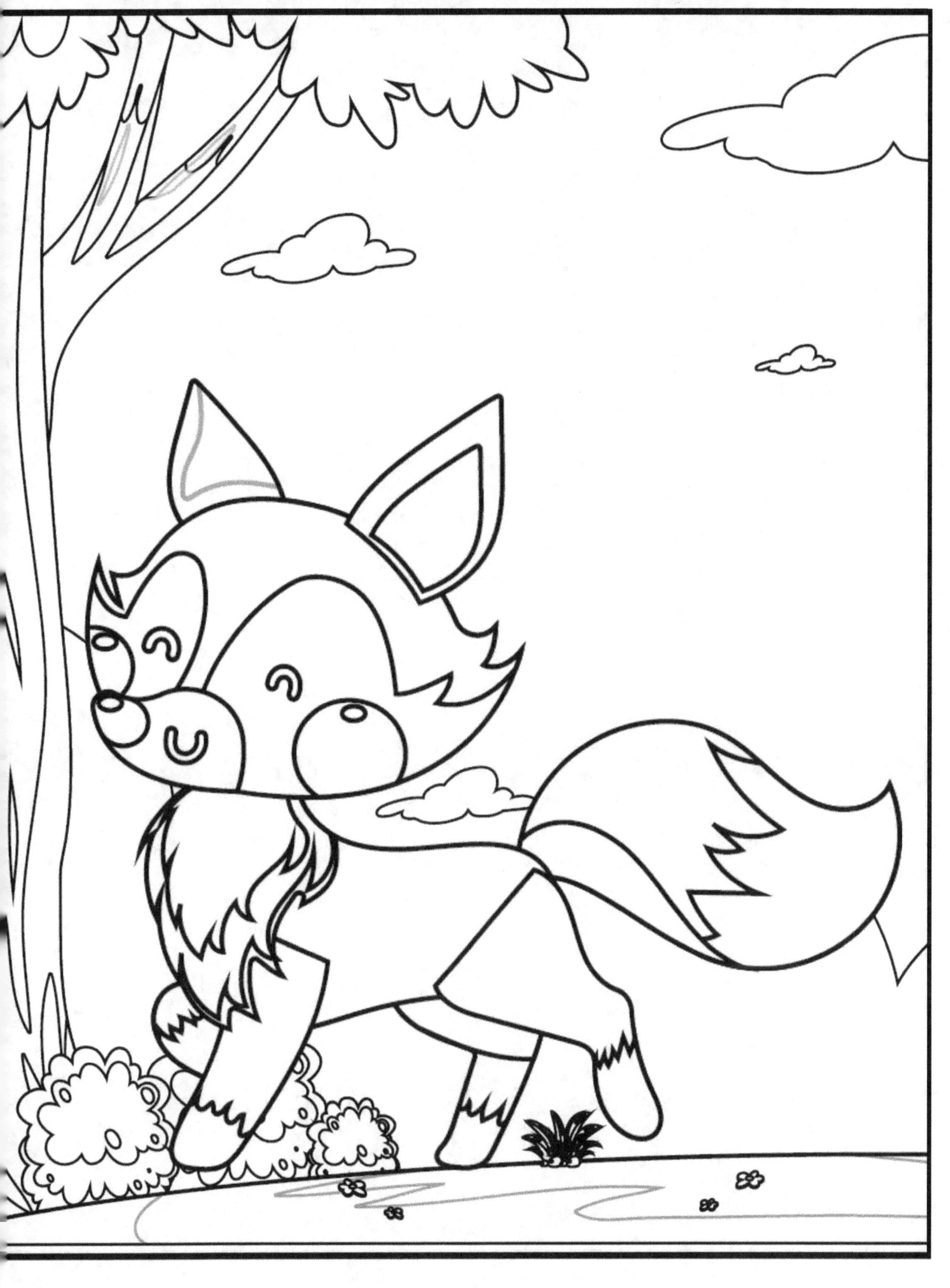

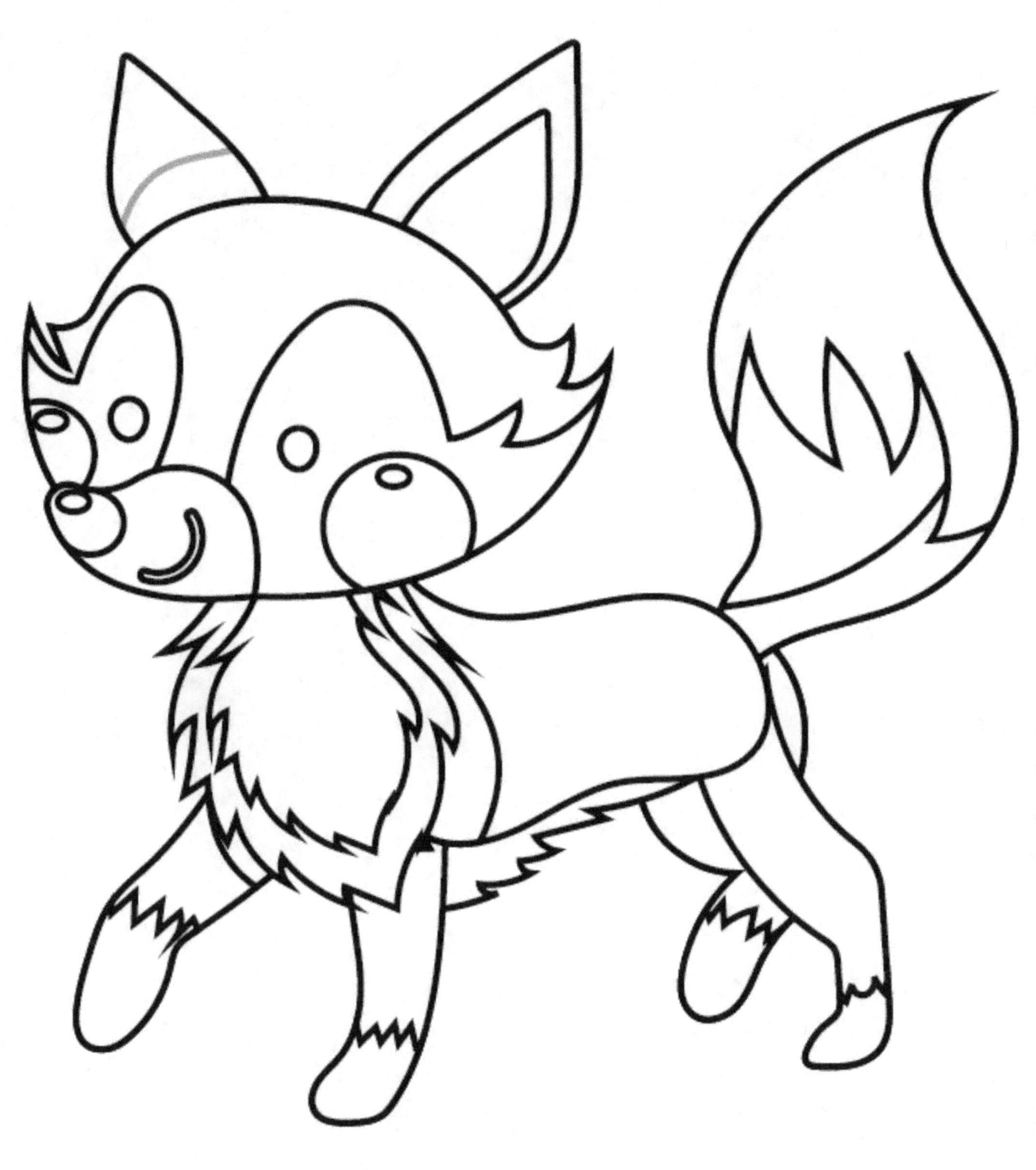

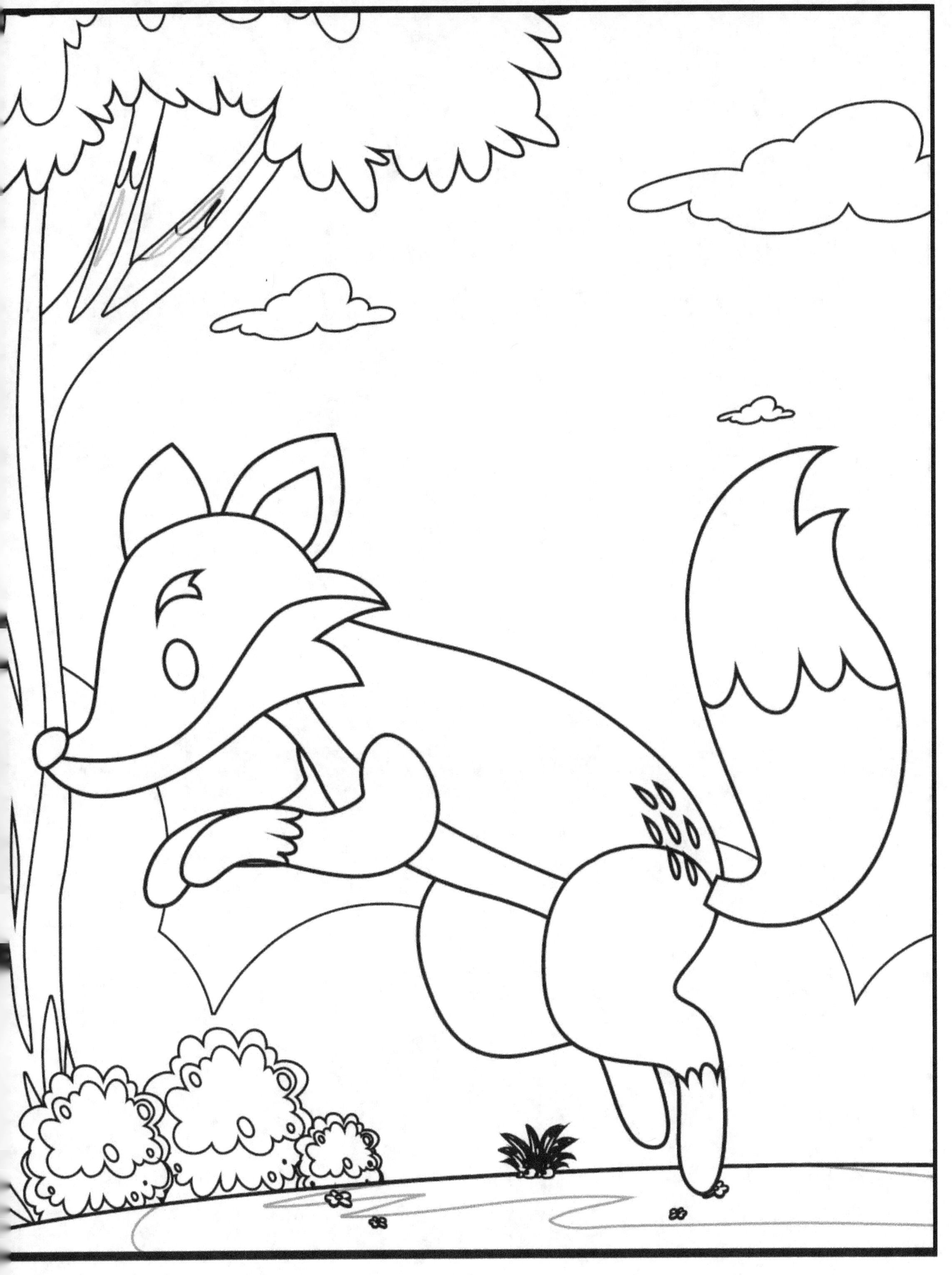

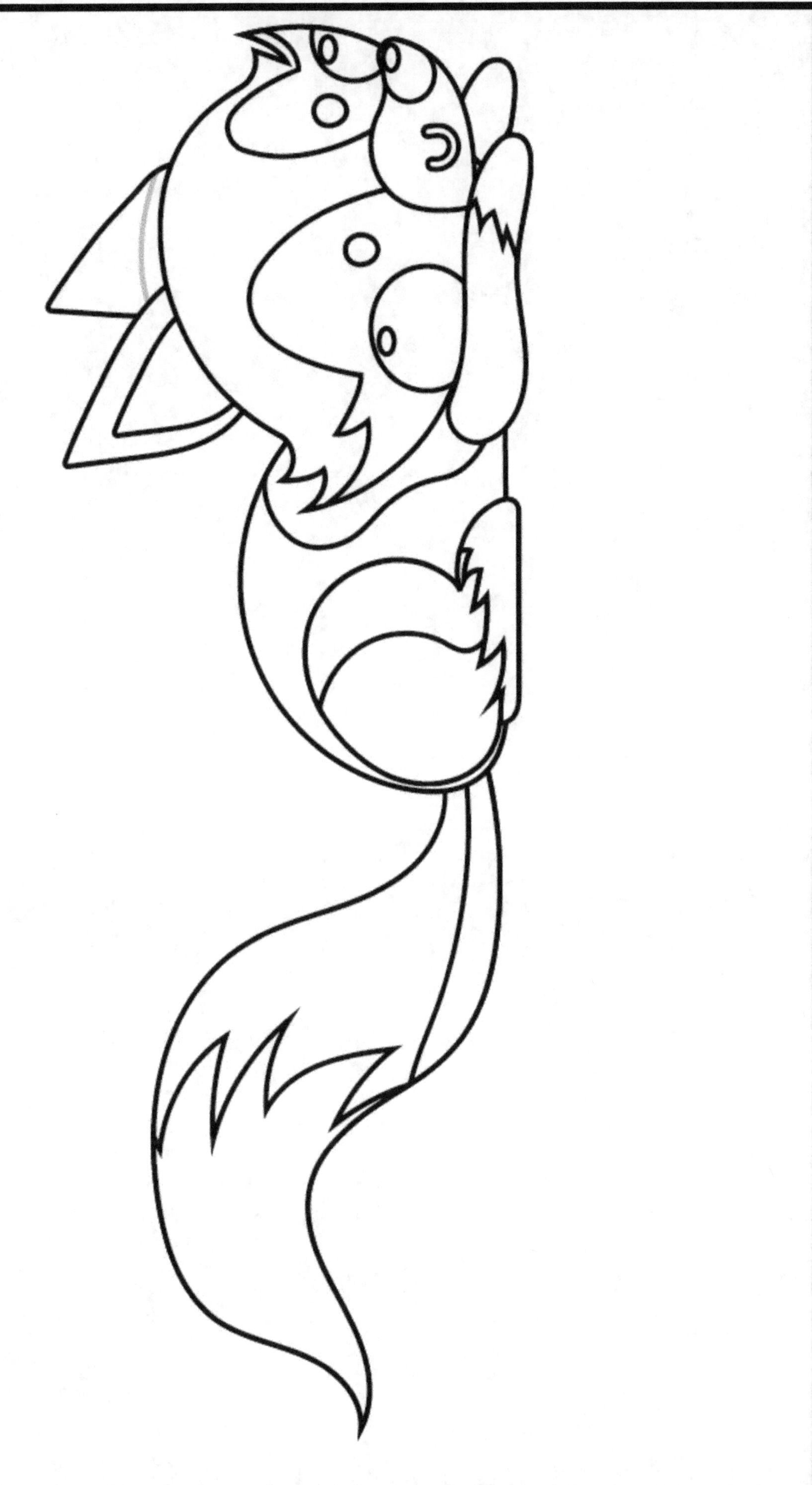

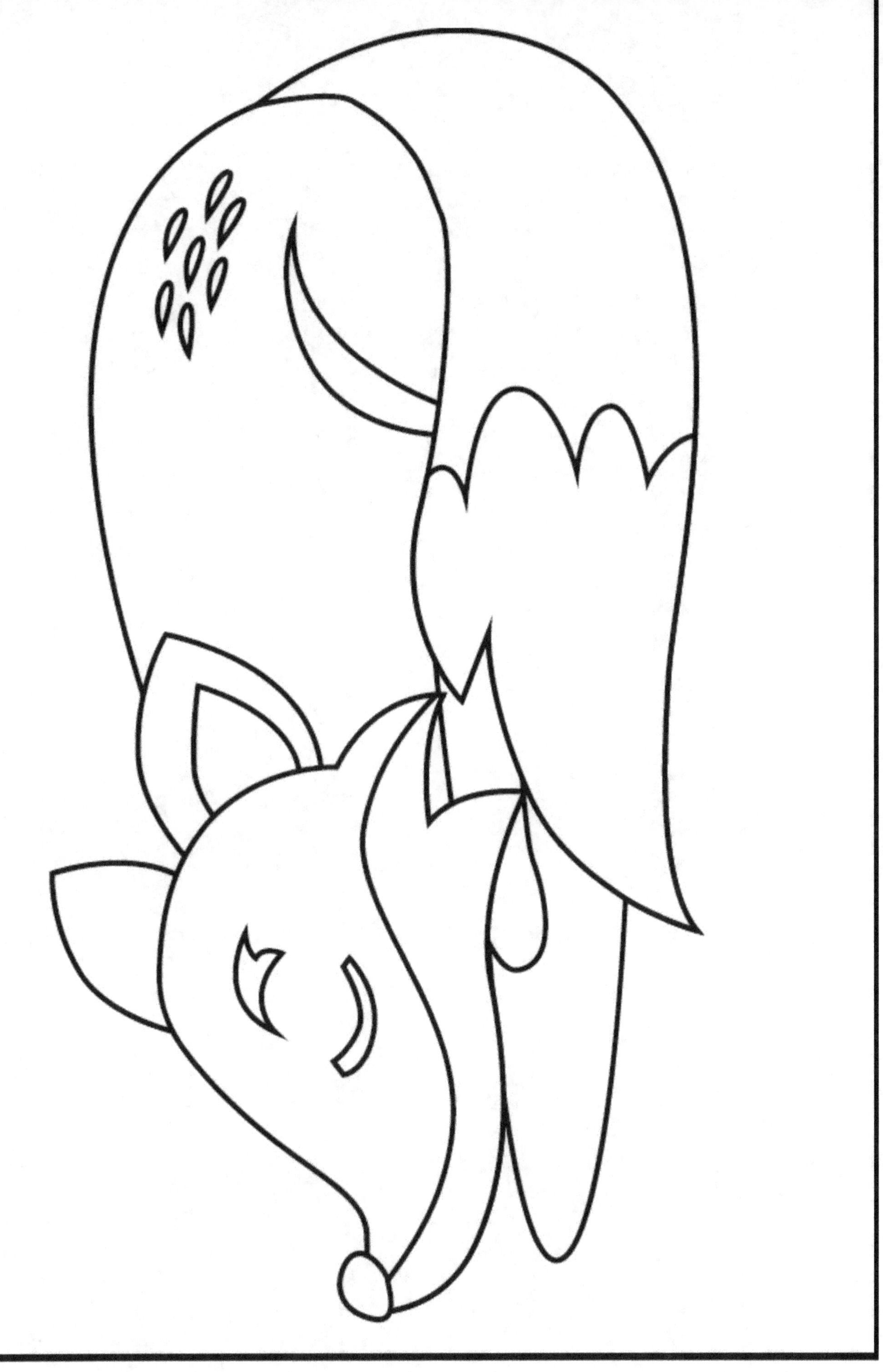

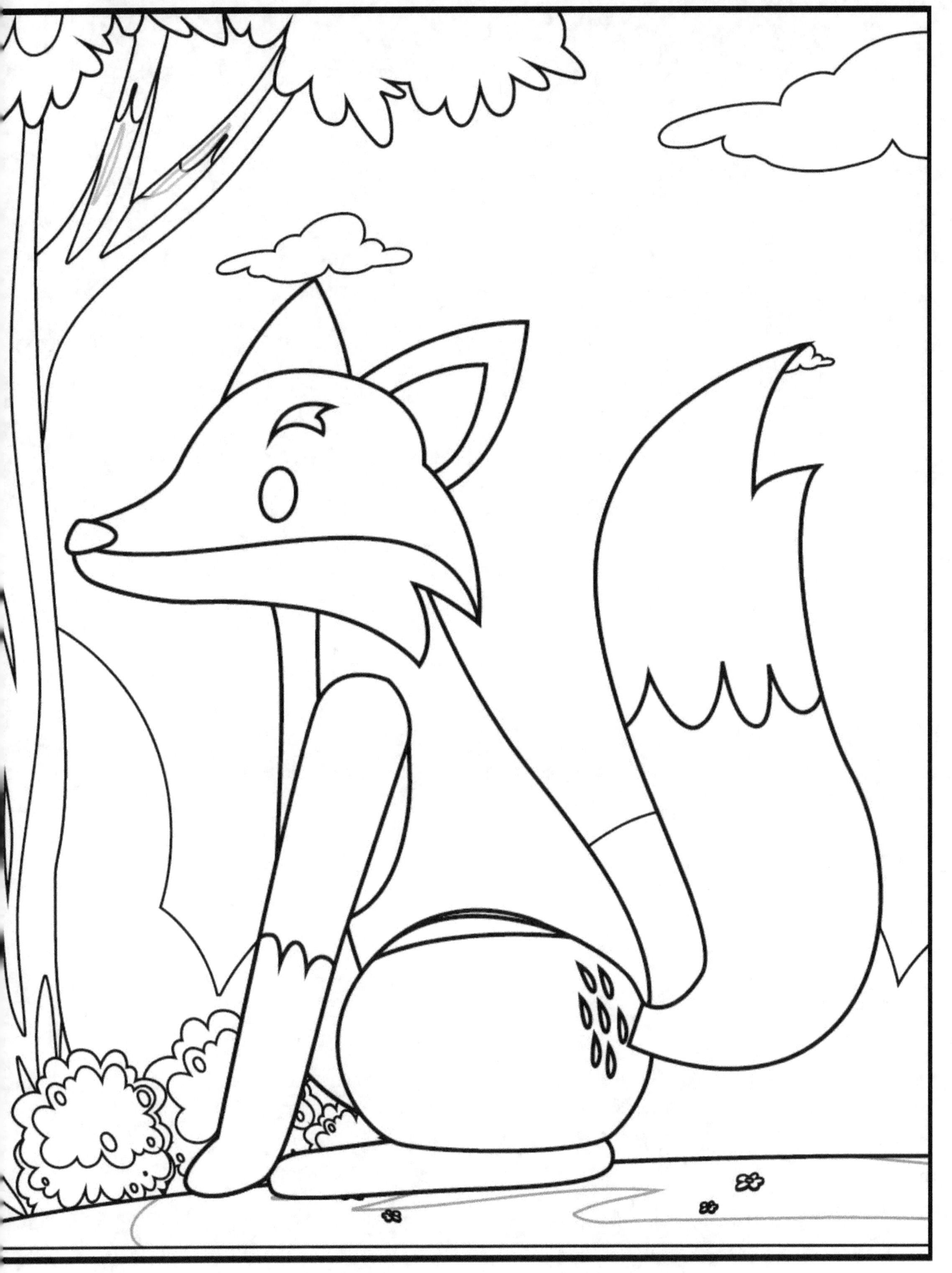

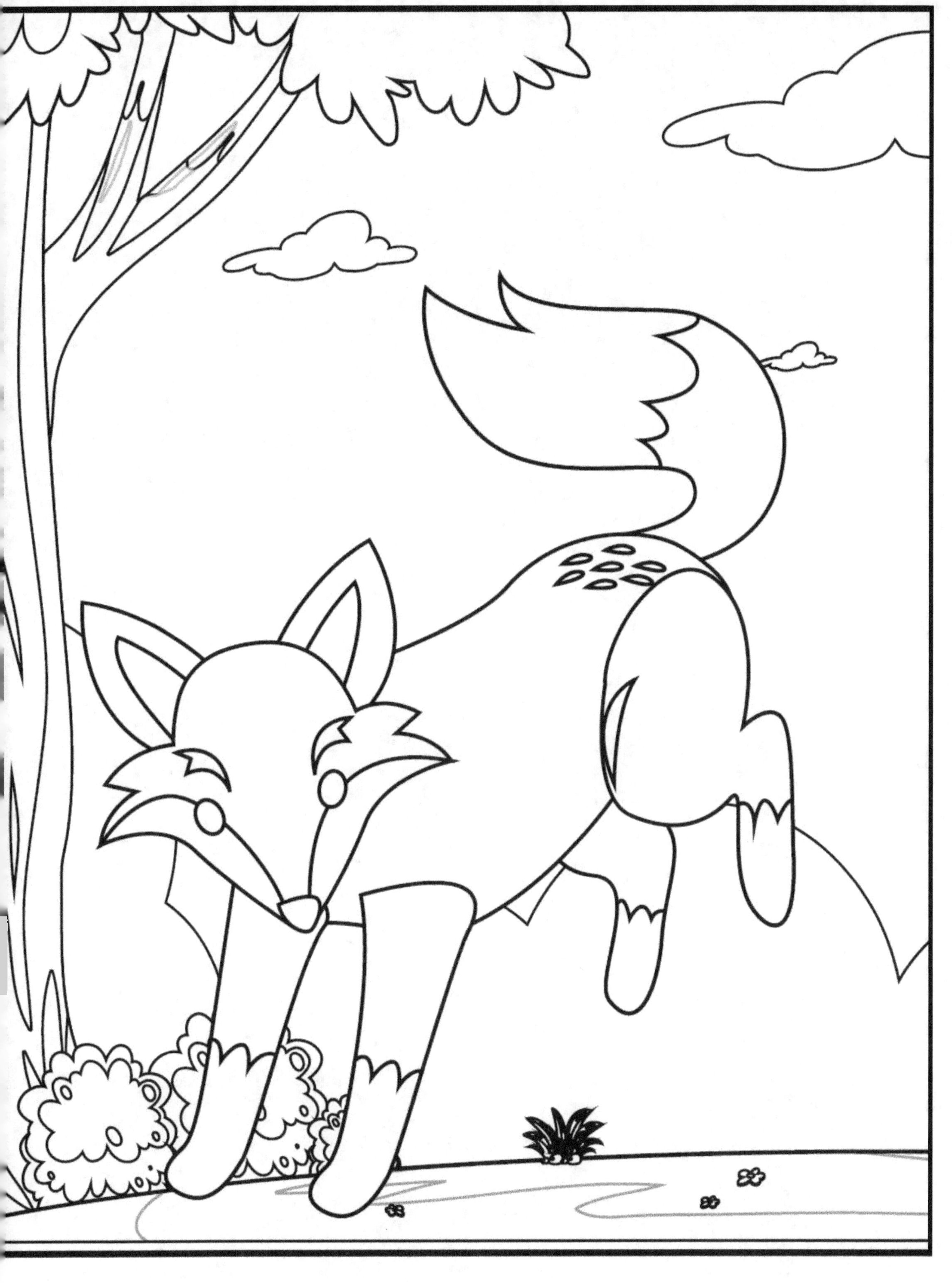

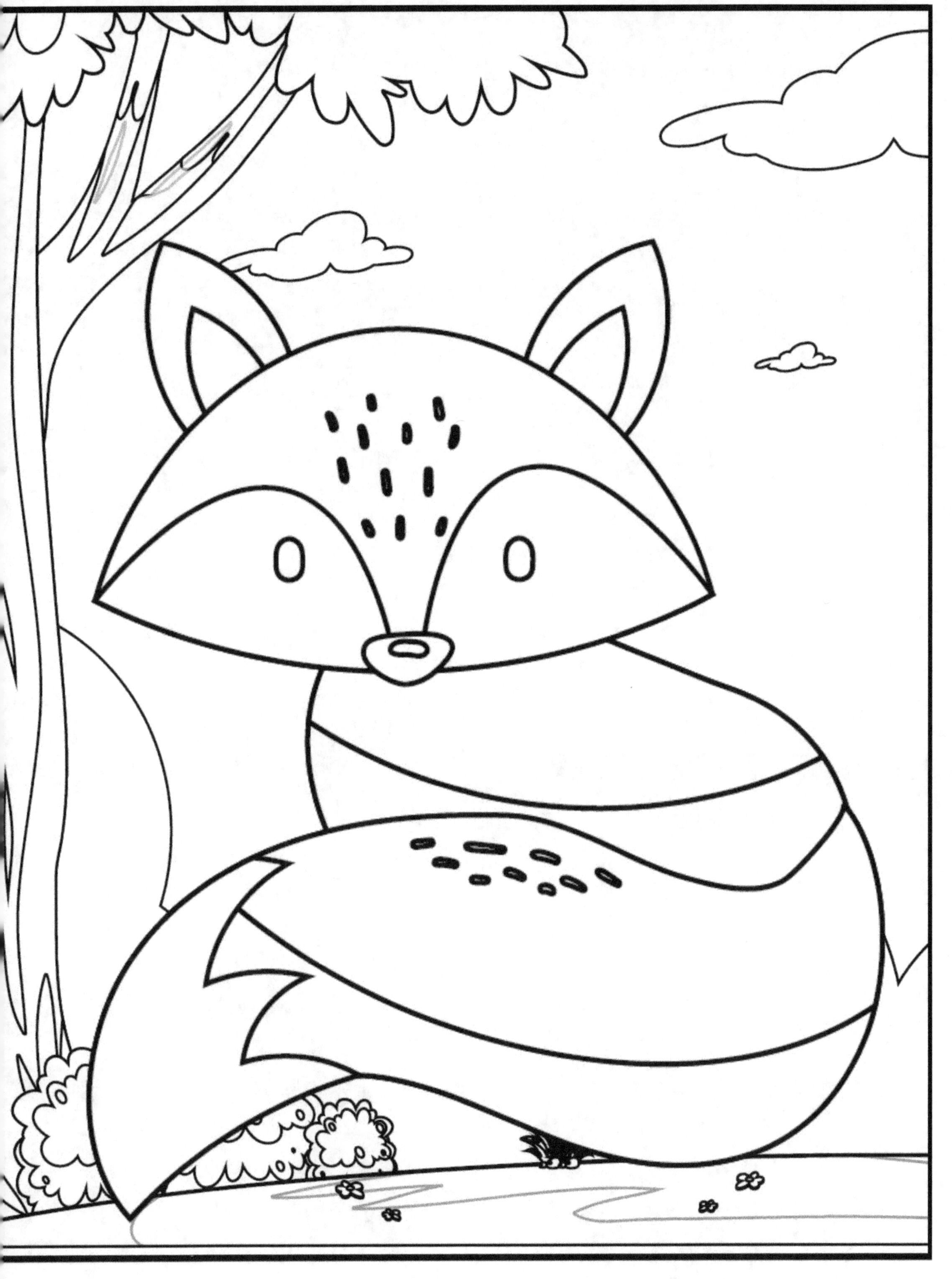

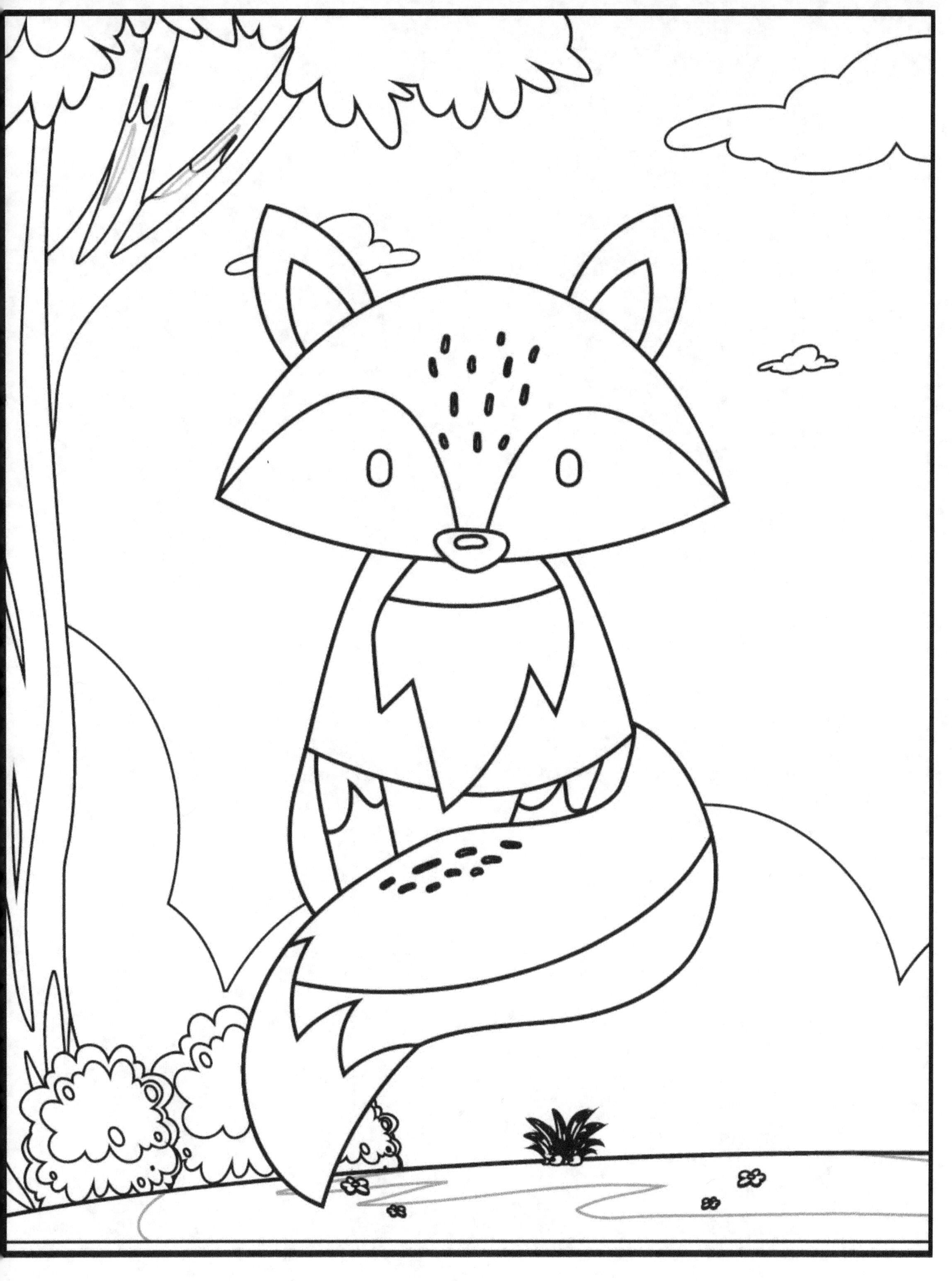

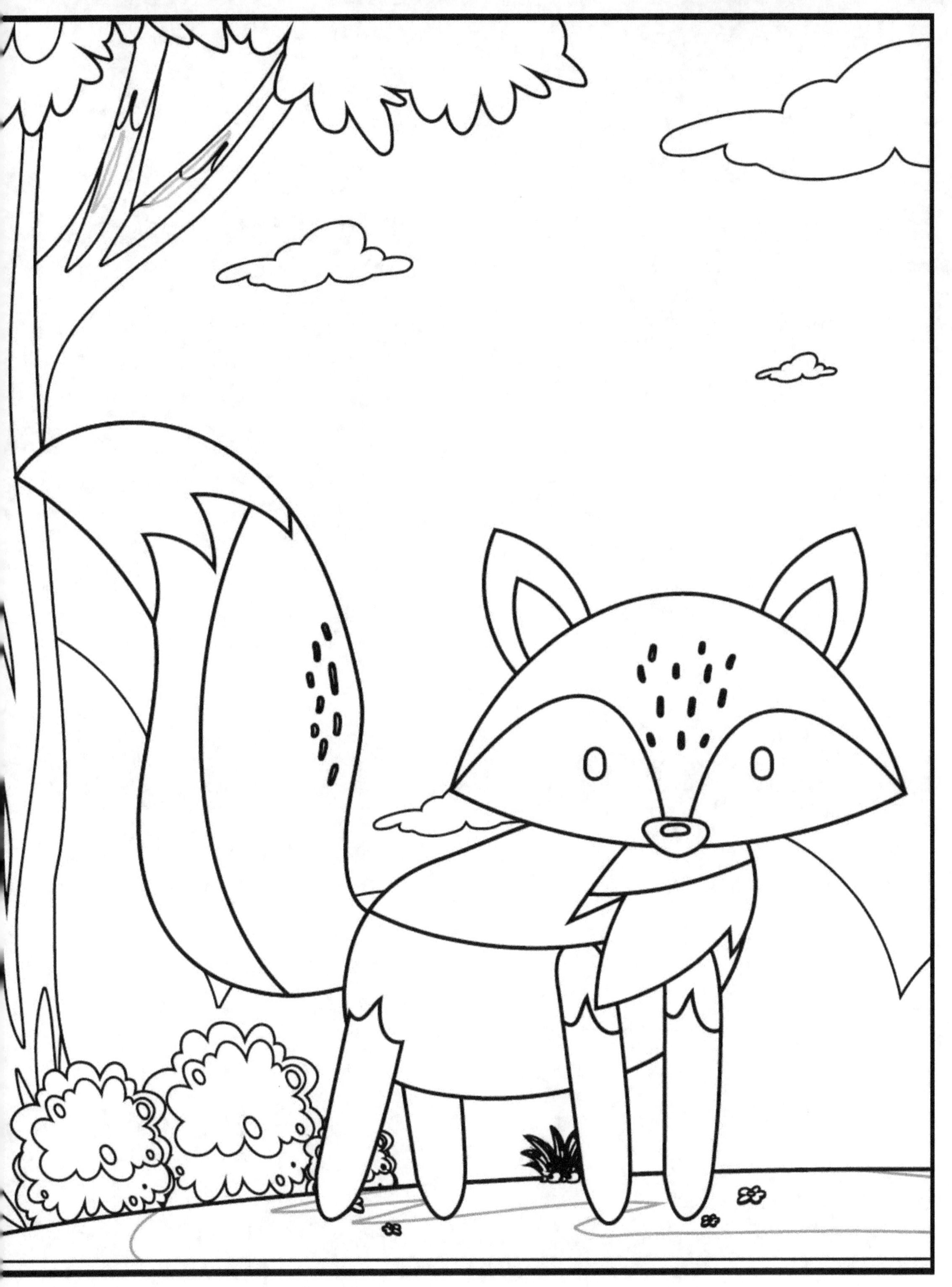

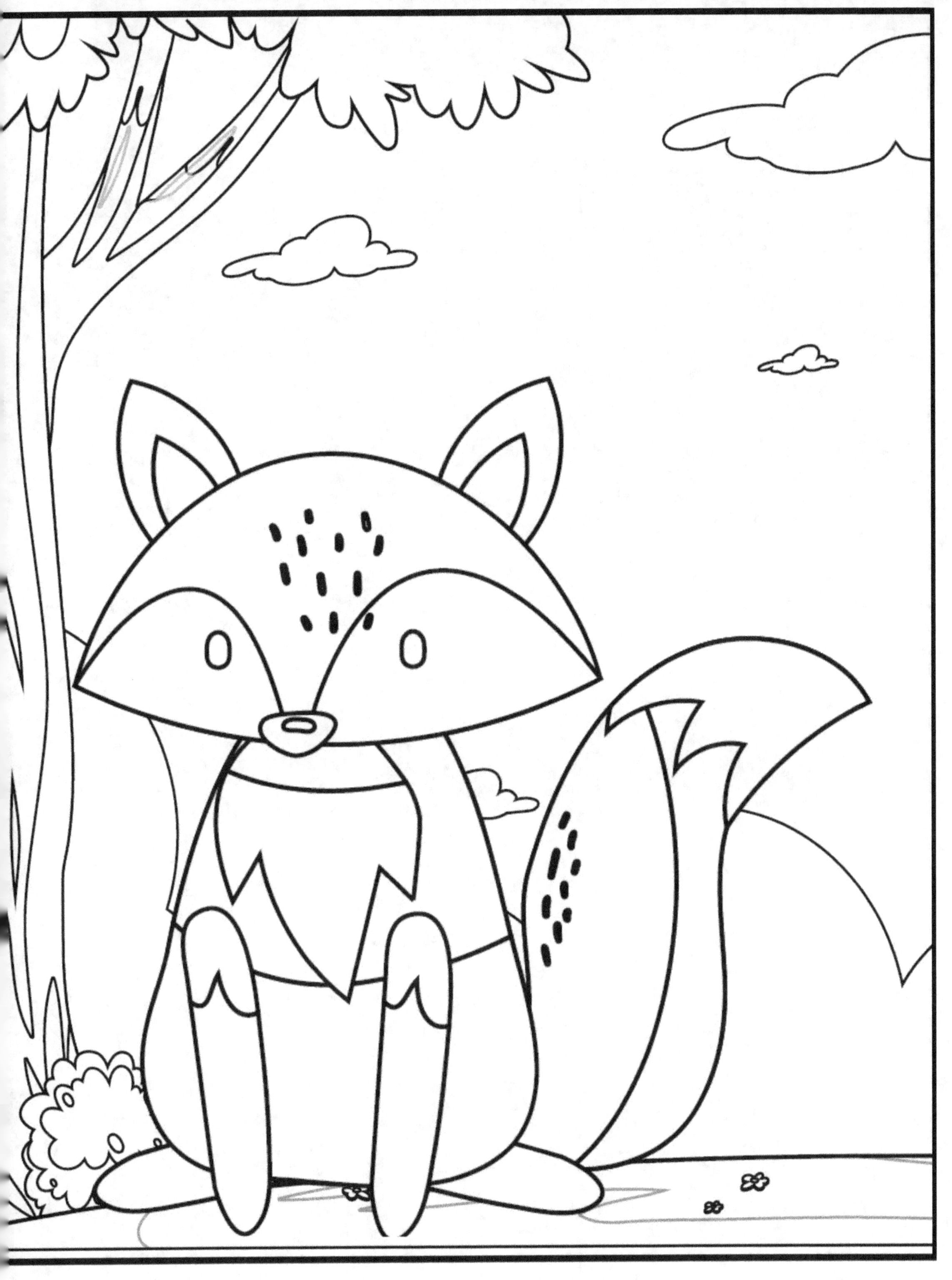

FOX

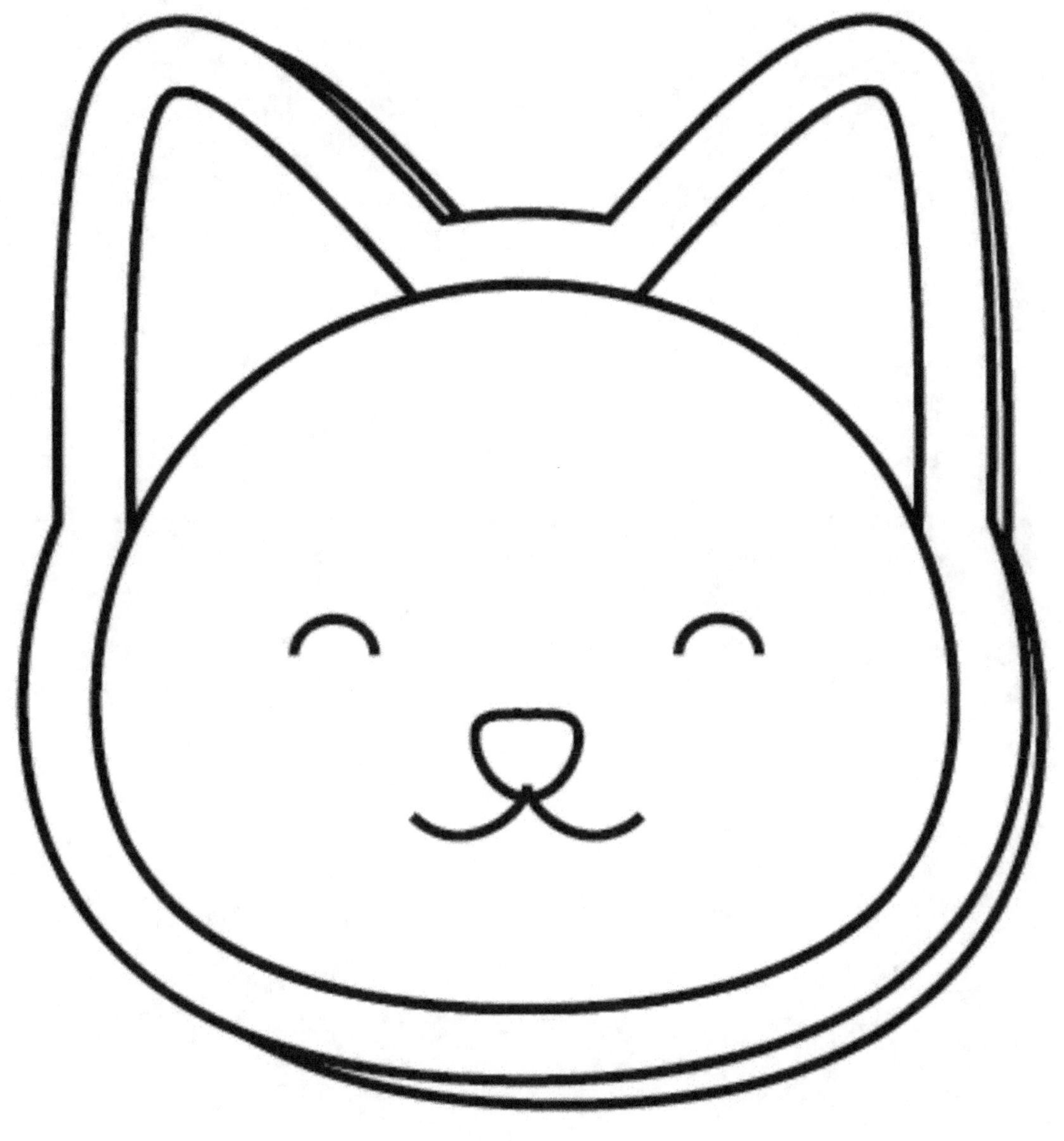

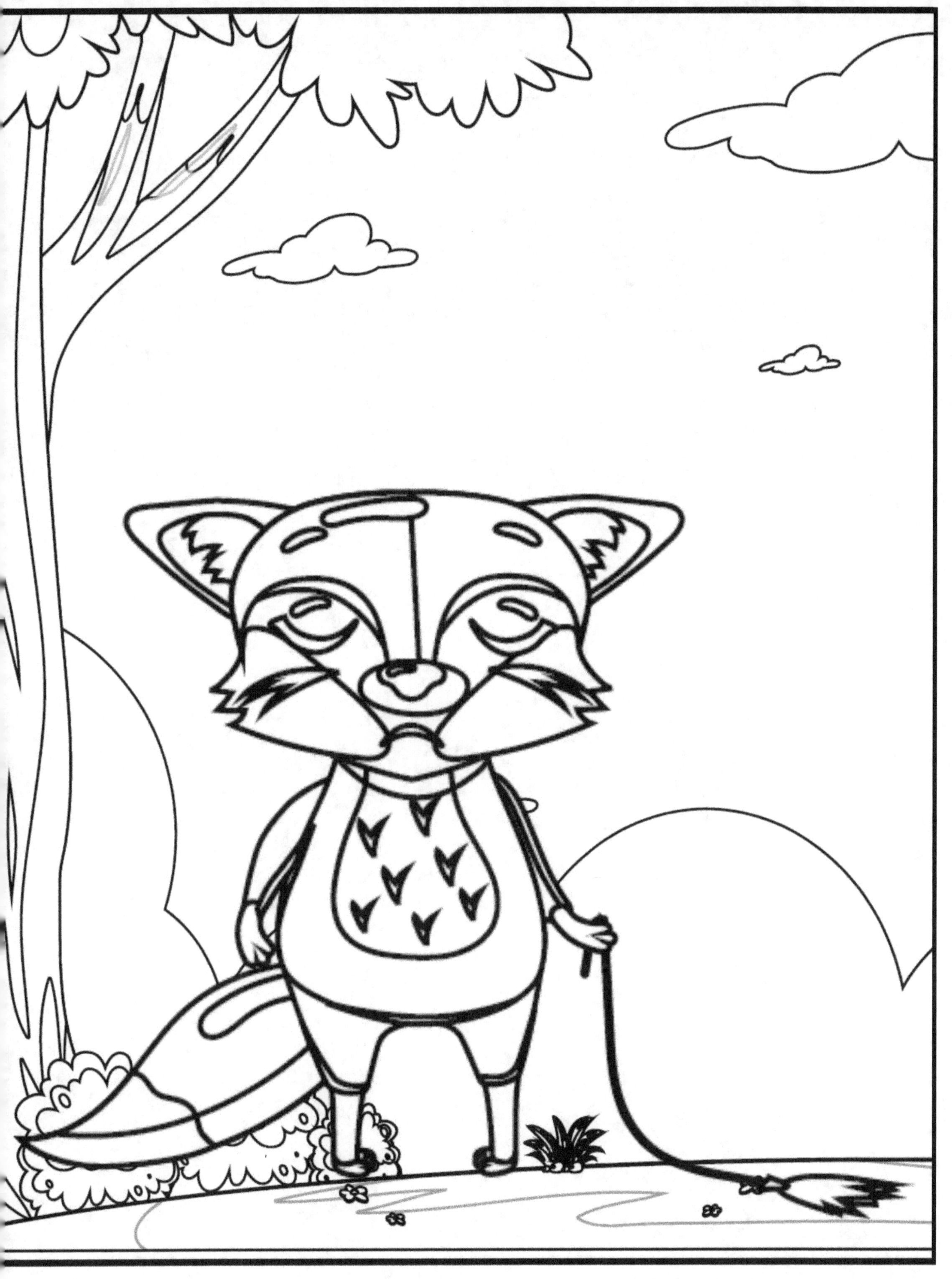

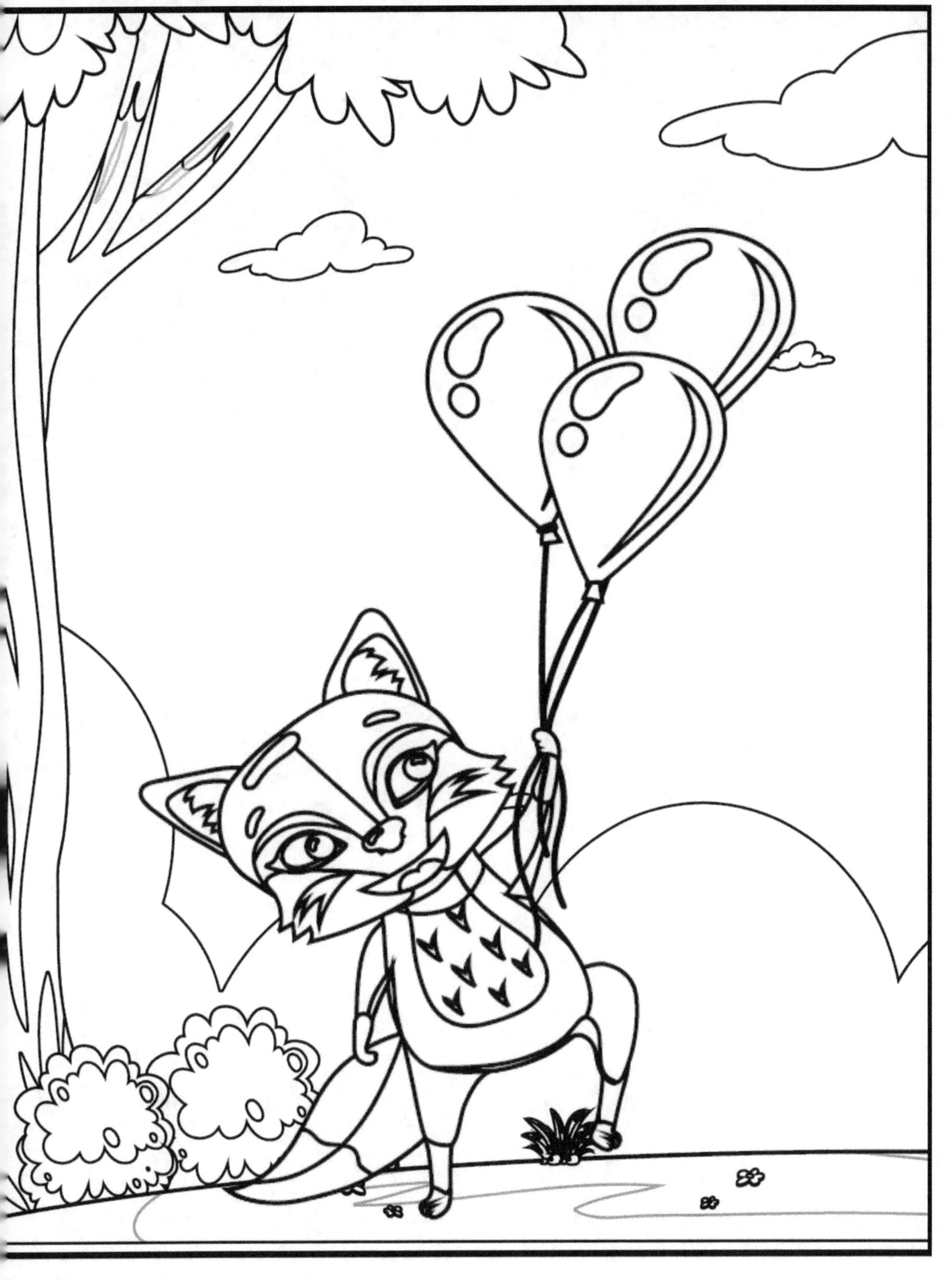

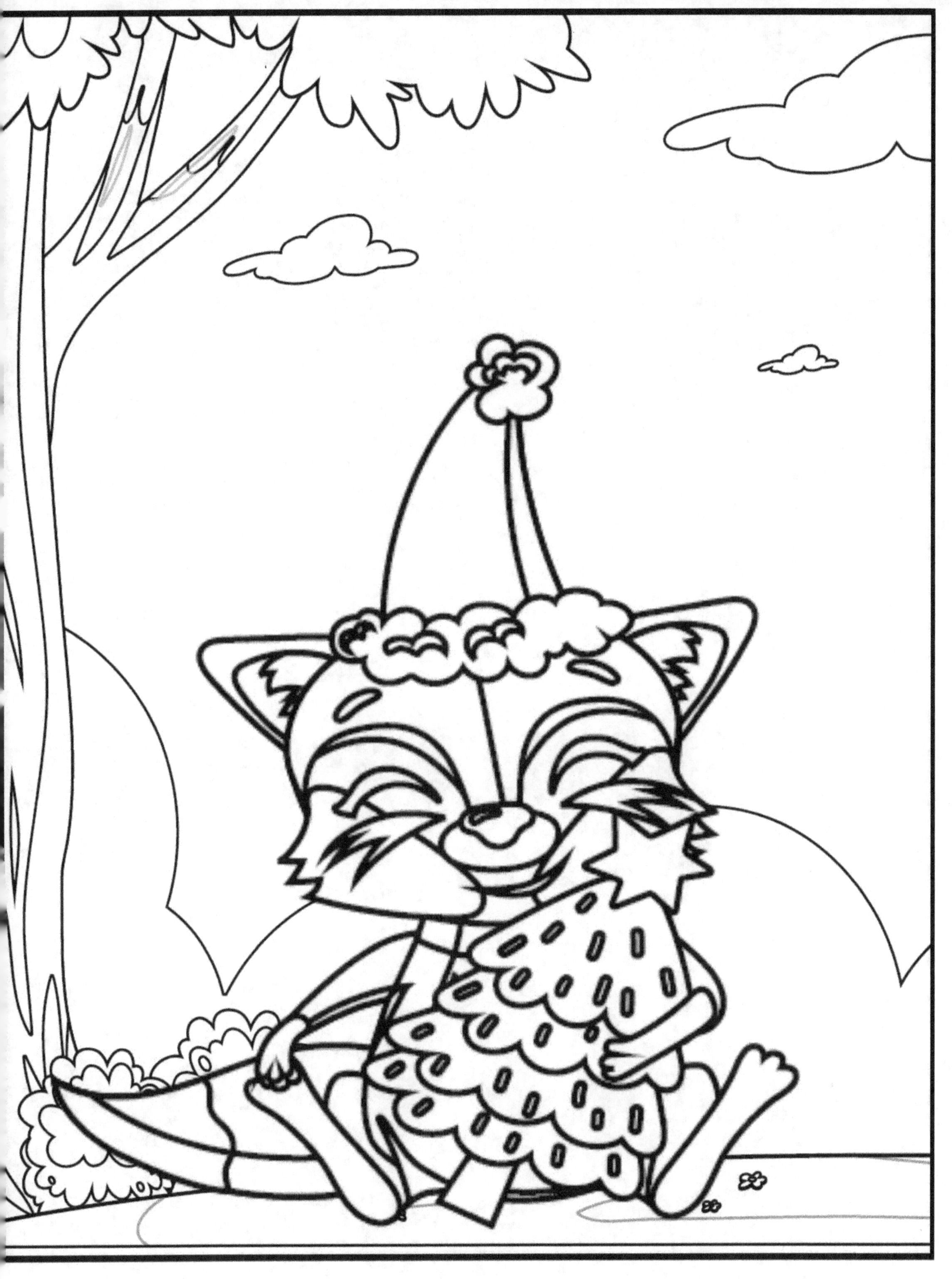

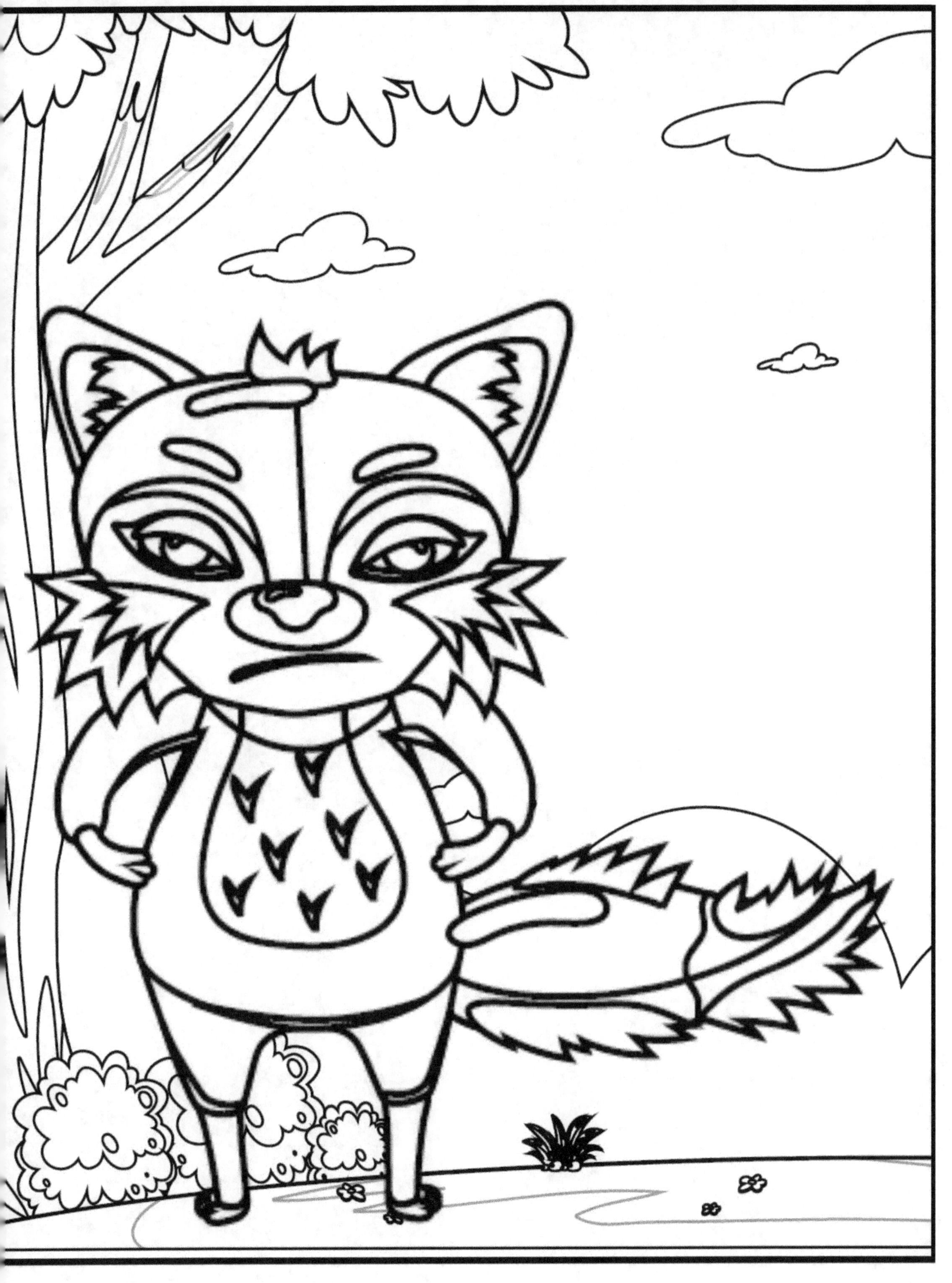

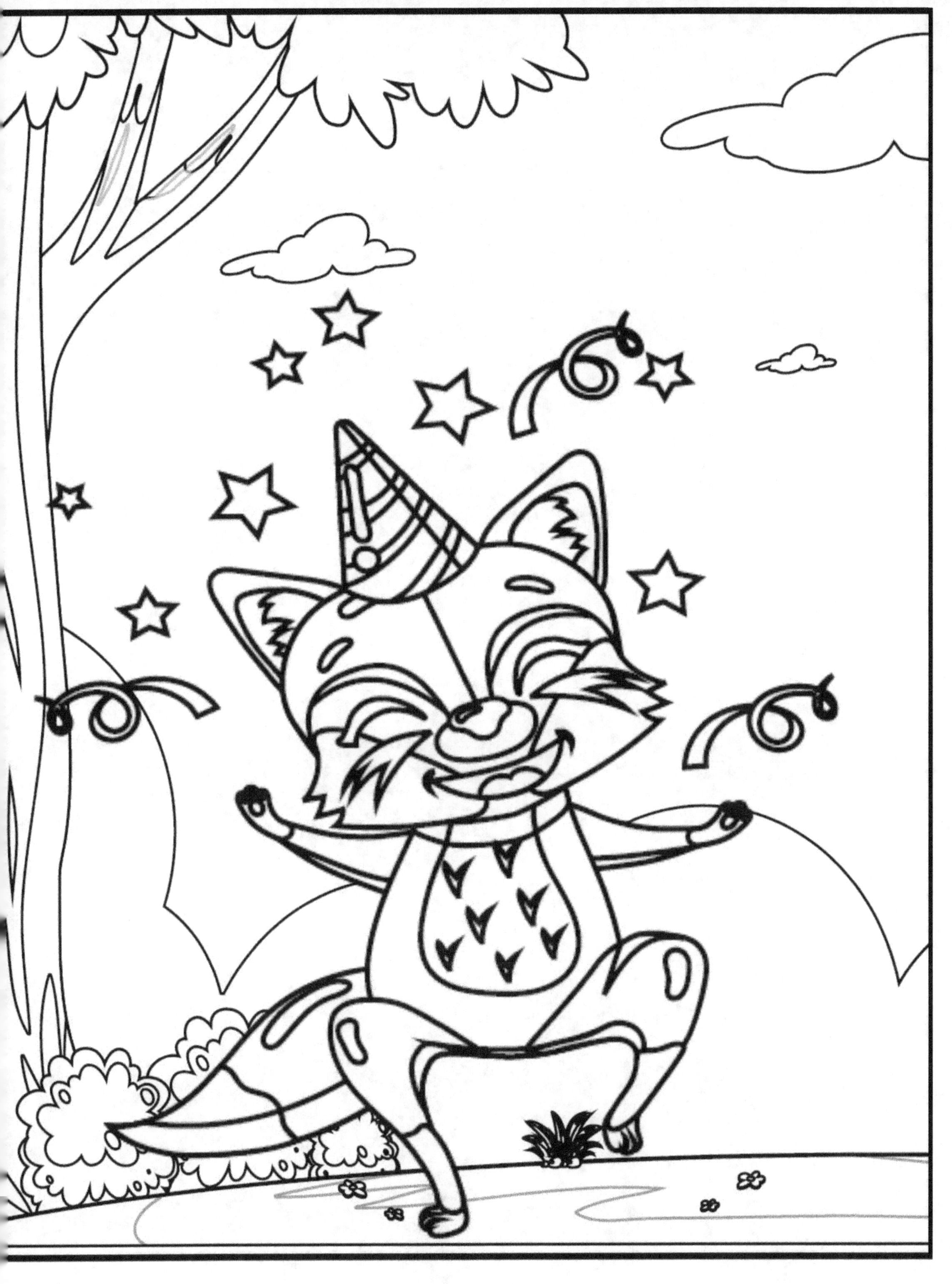

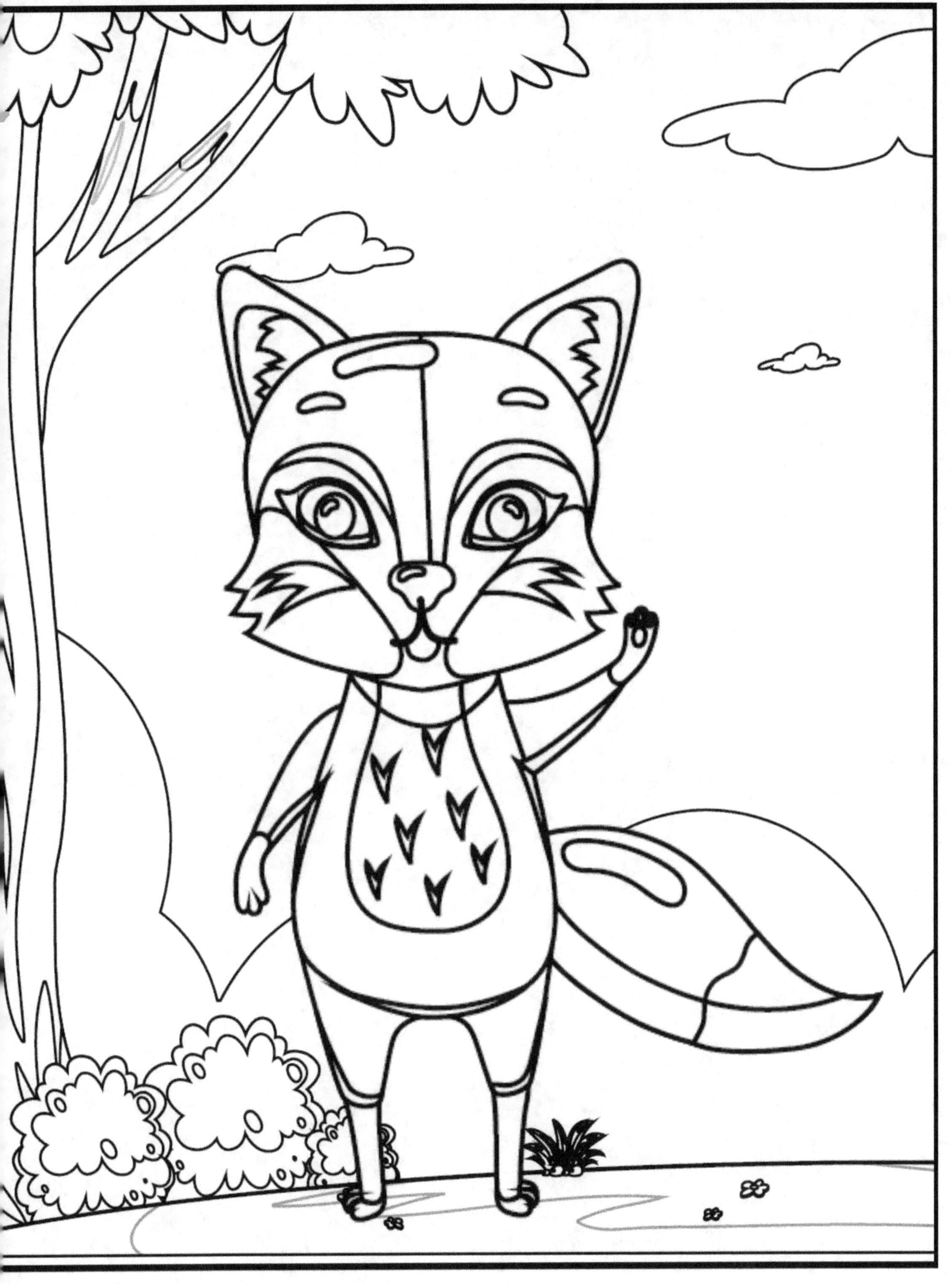

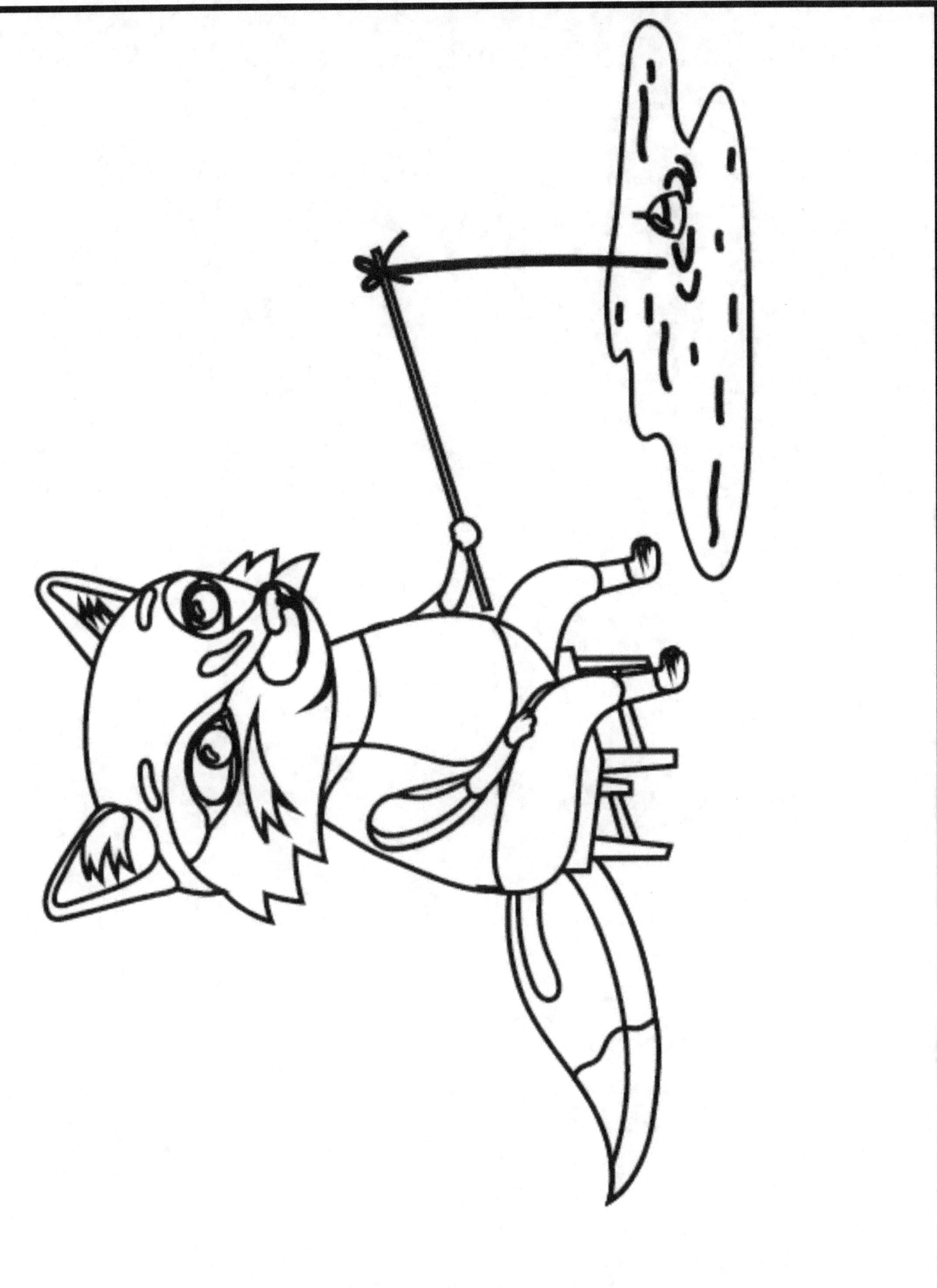

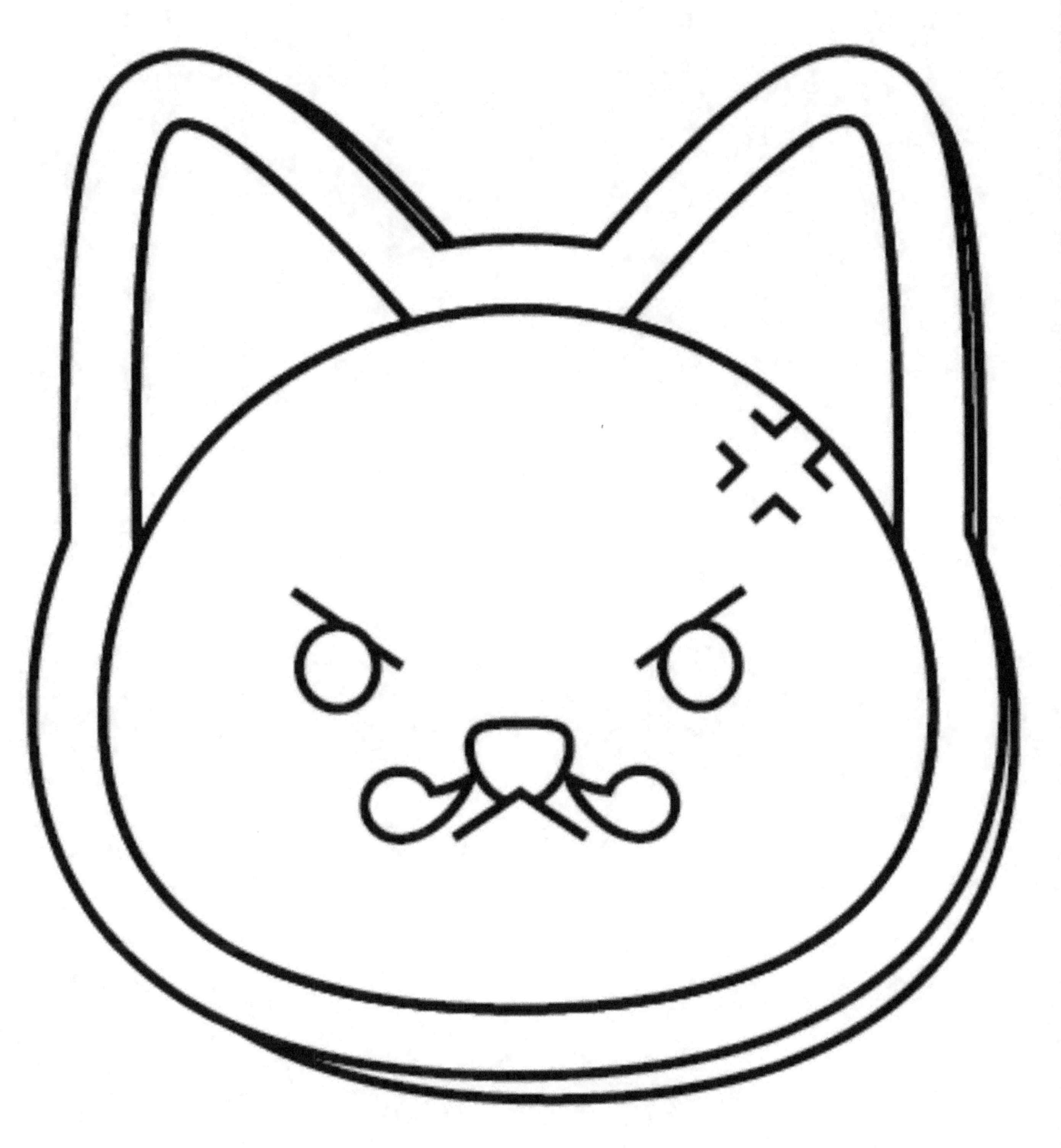

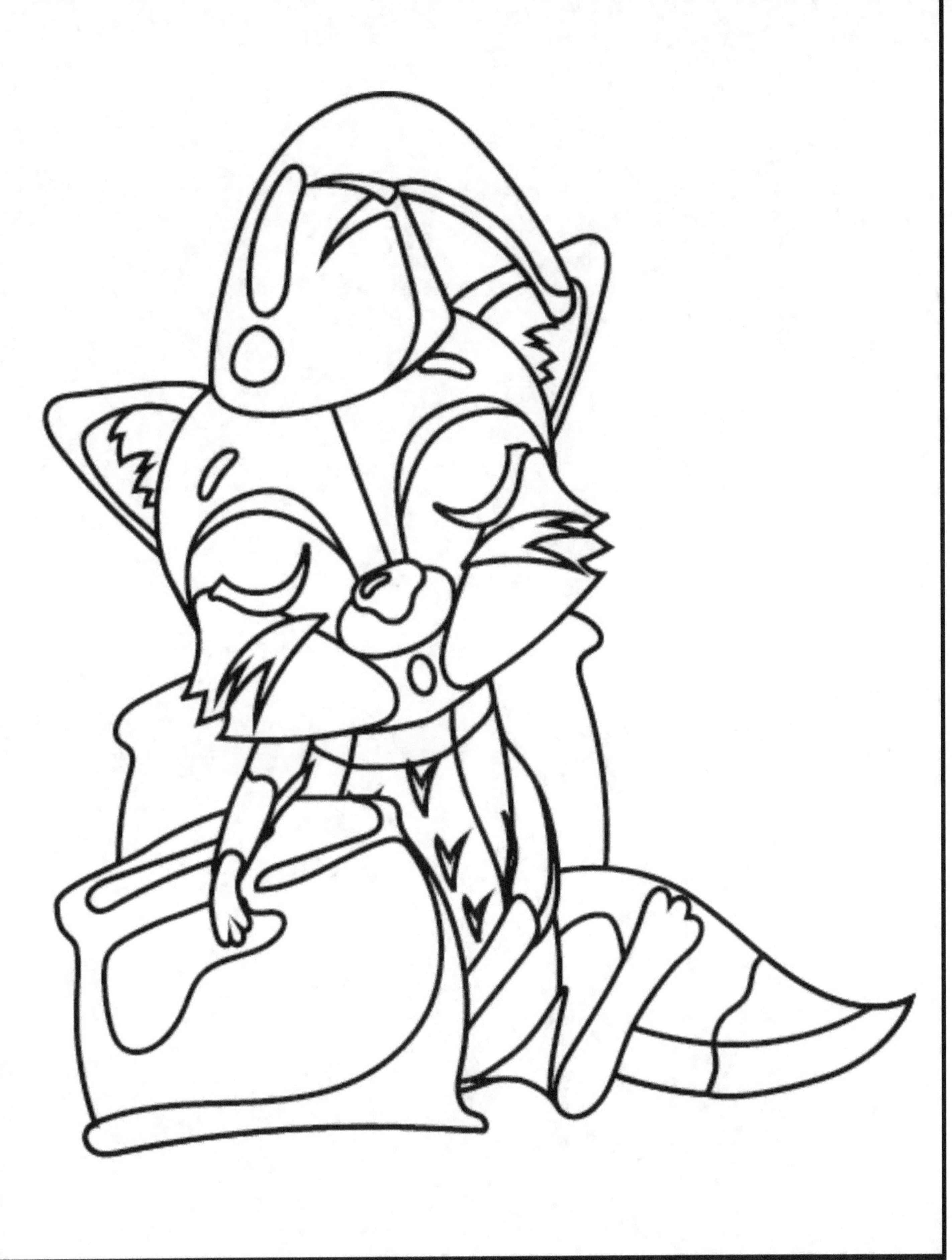

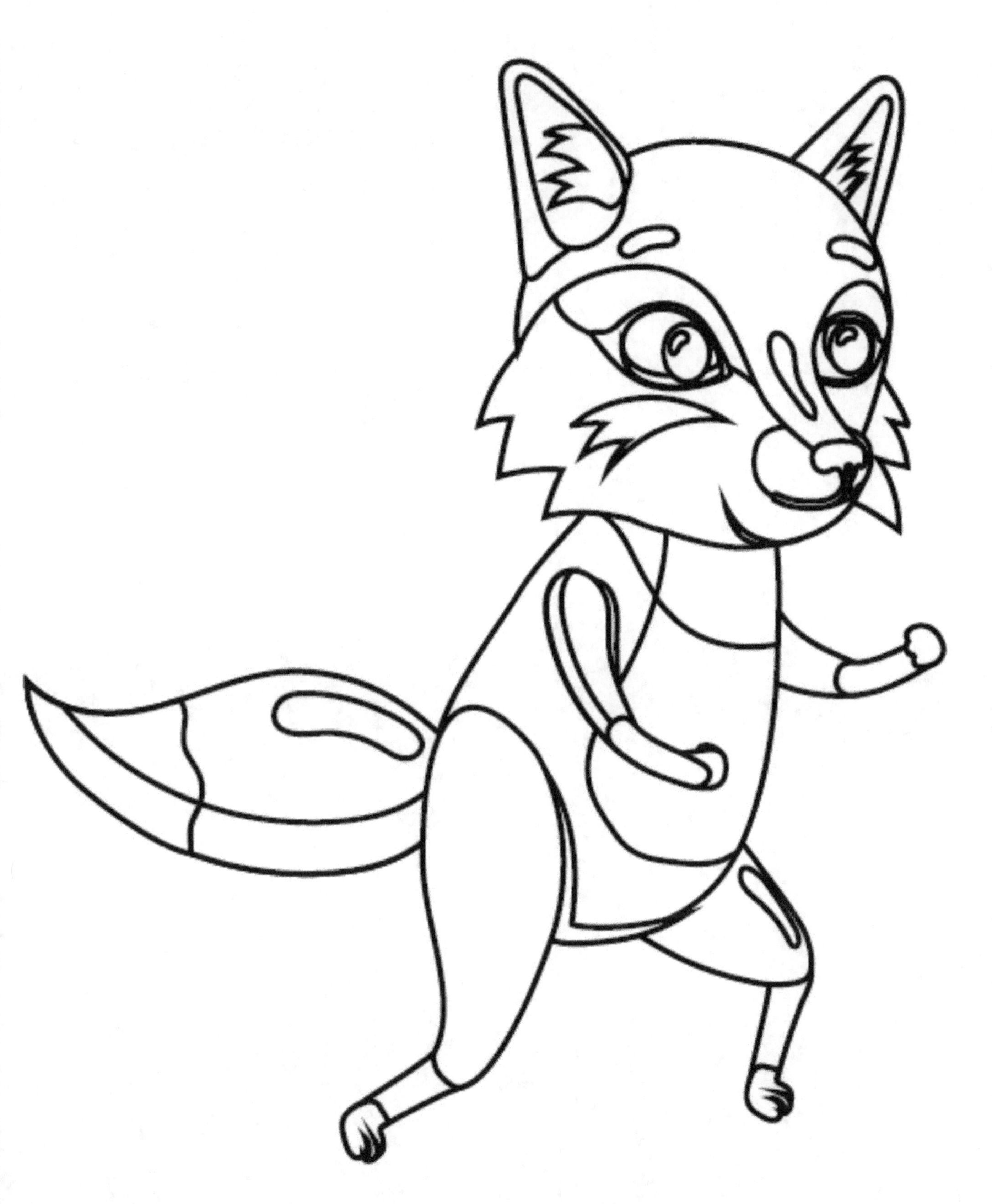

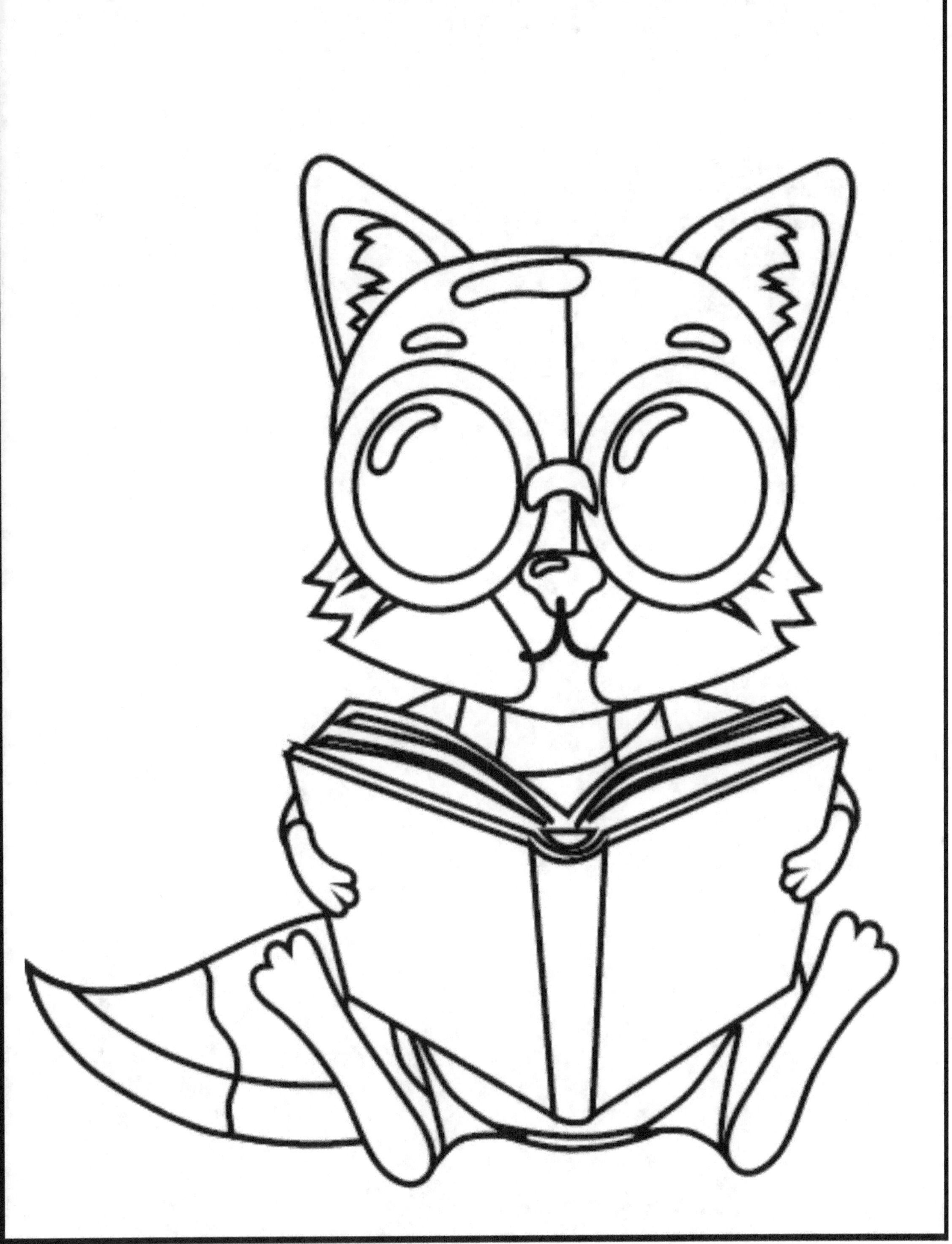

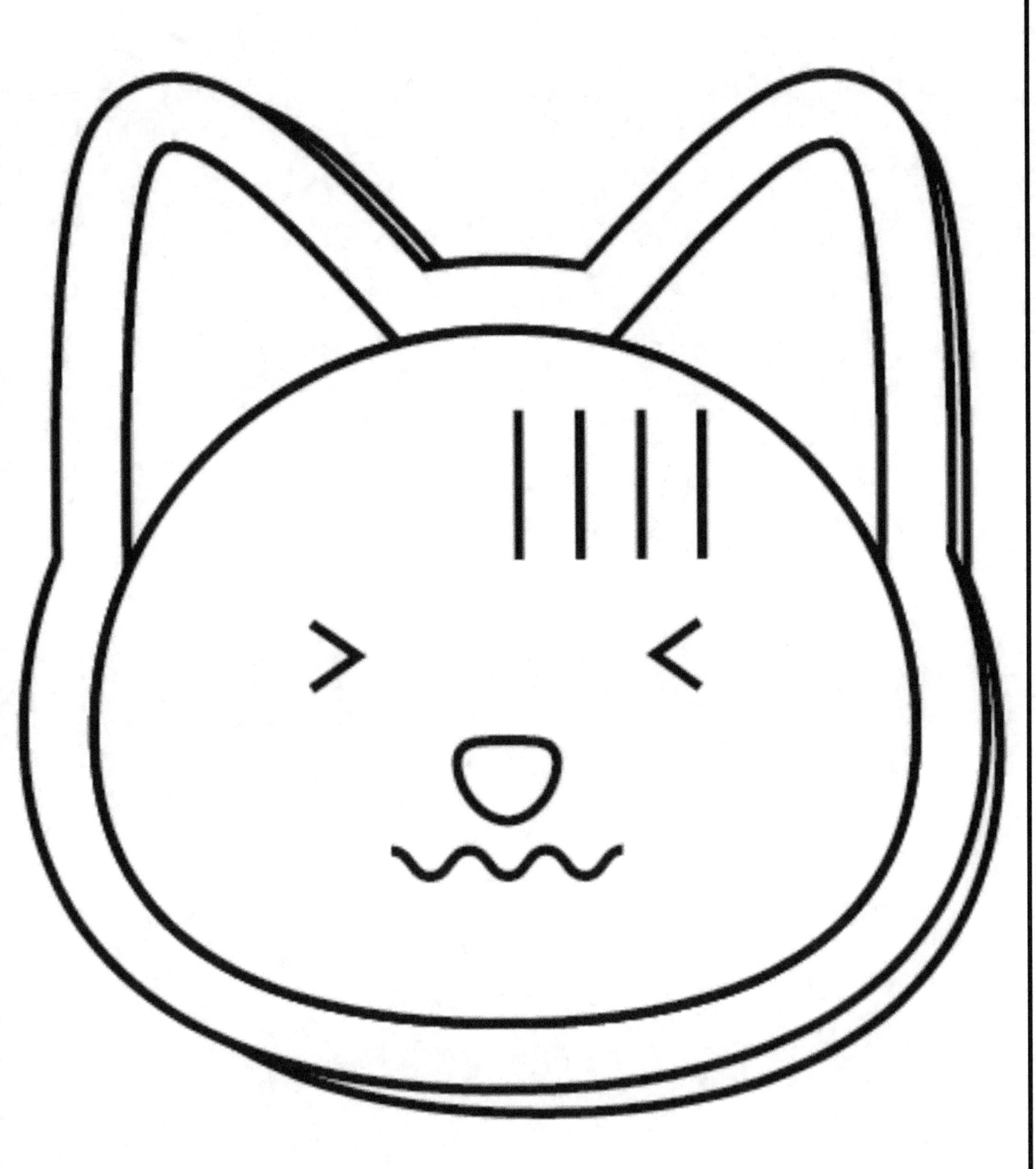

www.ingramcontent.com/pod-product-compliance
Lightning Source LLC
Chambersburg PA
CBHW081246250726
48654CB00012B/1502

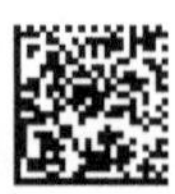

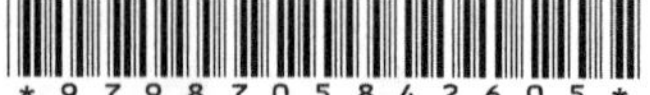